WALK INTO FREEDOM

CHRISTIAN OUTREACH TO PEOPLE INVOLVED
IN COMMERCIAL SEXUAL EXPLOITATION

RUTH H. ROBB
AND
MARION L.S. CARSON

THE PEOPLE'S SEMINARY PRESS

Walk into Freedom
Christian Outreach to People Involved in Commercial Sexual Exploitation

Authors: Ruth H. Robb and Marion L.S. Carson
Forward : Lauran D. Bethell
Illustrations: Ian Smith

Copyright © 2020 *Ruth H. Robb and Marion L.S. Carson*. All rights reserved. Except for brief quotations in critical publications or reviews, no part of this publication may be reproduced in any manner without prior written permission from the publisher.

The People's Seminary Press
P.O. BOX 410
Burlington, WA 98233
www.peoplesseminary.org

ISBN paperback: 978-1-954387-01-0
ISBN e-book: 978-1-954387-02-7

All Scripture quotations, unless otherwise indicated, are taken from the Holy Bible, New International Version®, NIV®. Copyright ©1973, 1978, 1984, 2011 by Biblica, Inc.™ Used by permission of Zondervan. All rights reserved worldwide. www.zondervan.com. The "NIV" and "New International Version" are trademarks registered in the United States Patent and Trademark Office by Biblica, Inc.™

Made in the USA.

FOR CARMEL,
who "just" gets on with it

Contents

	Foreword	vii
	Preface	ix
Chapter 1	Commercial Sexual Exploitation: The Basics	1
Chapter 2	The Bigger Picture	11
Chapter 3	What does the Bible have to say?	21
Chapter 4	Starting a Ministry	29
Chapter 5	Outreach and Relationships	39
Chapter 6	Leadership and Teamwork	51
Chapter 7	Management and Governance	61
Chapter 8	Resilience in Ministry	71
Chapter 9	Exploitation, Violence and Abuse	83
Chapter 10	Health and Illness	93
Chapter 11	Mental Health Problems	103
Chapter 12	Addiction	113
Chapter 13	Exiting, Recovery and Rehabilitation	123
Chapter 14	Discipleship	133
Chapter 15	Spiritual Matters	143
	Epilogue	155
	Further Reading	157

Foreword

BY LAURAN BETHELL

I KNOW THAT when Ruth Robb began working with people in prostitution in the 1980's, she had no "how to" manual to turn to! She only knew that God had called her to be with women who were considered outcasts and sinners, and meet them in Jesus' name and with his love. The women were her teachers, her social work degree provided a theoretical framework, and God was her Guide and Wisdom, as she pioneered ministries that God has exponentially used to redeem countless lives.

Marion Carson was a psychiatric nurse, who did a PhD in Biblical studies and combined forces with Ruth in one of her early outreach projects with women. It was a time when God's Spirit was being poured out on this world, calling people in many cities and towns to shine the Light of God's Love into the dark corners where so many were trapped in prostitution. Ruth and Marion knew that people were desperate for information—for a "how to" for reaching this challenging population, and their first book *Working the Streets* was written. It was ground-breaking—and provided practical information available no-where else about setting up ministry for people in prostitution. It was rooted in psychological research, theological depth and pointed the reader towards public services and resources available in the UK. Most importantly, it was based on years of their personal experiences, having worked with countless numbers of survivors of commercial sexual exploitation.

Fast forward a couple of decades: in these intervening years, Ruth's and Marion's expertise has been extensively called upon in the international sphere, and it became clear that a new, more expansive book was needed. *Walk Into Freedom* is a research and experienced based dive into the wide-world of ministry with women who are being commercially sexually exploited—especially written for those anywhere in the world who have ever asked the question "Are you calling *me* to *do something?*" The reader is engaged through true-to-life case studies, presented in story-style, that develop and deepen as the book moves along. Each chapter ends with a Bible study and thought-provoking questions. Ruth and Marion use global examples and point to a wealth of resources for follow-up. It's the best "how-to" manual there is for becoming involved in ministry with people in prostitution because it's written by smart women who know their stuff because they've lived every word of it.

Read this book at your own risk. It's a subject that most would rather avoid. But if you want God to speak deeply into your heart and equip you to join a profoundly life-altering movement, then *Walk Into Freedom* is the place to begin the journey.

God's Grace and Peace Be with You,
Rev. Dr. Lauran Bethell
Global Consultant,
Responses to Human Trafficking
International Ministries ABC/USA
Coordinator,
International Christian Alliance on Prostitution (ICAP)

Preface

Walk with me and work with me—watch how I do it. Learn the unforced rhythms of grace. I won't lay anything heavy or ill-fitting on you. Keep company with me and you'll learn to live freely and lightly.
Matthew 11:29-30 (The Message)

THIS BOOK CONTAINS information and advice for Christians who want to reach out to those involved in commercial sexual exploitation. It draws on many years' experience of working in this area in the UK and beyond. Ruth is an activist and international consultant. She is co-founder and CEO of Azalea, a charity based in Luton, England which reaches out to and helps people to leave commercial sexual exploitation. Ruth is also on the leadership team of the International Christian Alliance on Prostitution, representing Europe. Marion is a theologian and writer, who serves as Chaplain to Glasgow City Mission in Glasgow, Scotland.

This is not the first time we have written on this topic. In in 2004 New Wine Press published our book *Working the Streets: A Handbook for Christians involved in Outreach to Prostitutes*. We are delighted that this book has been, and still is, used extensively by teams throughout the world. Since then, however, we have grown a lot and learned a lot and we want to share something of this knowledge and experience with others. To that extent, many of the tips and hints found in *Working the Streets* are included here, but there is considerably more material, and more theological reflection. We have introduced Bible Study passages and questions for discussion, and illustrations by the Scottish artist, Ian Smith. We have told many stories which draw on our own experiences and those of people whom we have met and worked with. In every case, names have been changed. We have also tried to make the material more international in scope. However, we are fully aware that we cannot provide a "one size fits all" guidebook, and we hope that teams will be able to adapt the material as appropriate, in accordance with the cultural and legal constraints of the setting in which they are working.

Two things need to be said about language used in this book. First, we have avoided using the term "prostitute", preferring to speak of women involved in commercial sexual exploitation. This is partly because of the stigma that is often attached to the word "prostitute", but it is principally because, as we explain in chapter 2, we believe that prostitution is the objectification and exploitation of women's bodies. While we acknowledge that not everyone accepts this view, all that we have seen over the years has convinced us that the vast majority of the women working on the streets, and in bars and clubs, are likely to be victims of coercion and control and that they have all, without exception, suffered untold physical psychological and physical harm as a result of their experiences.

Second, throughout the book we speak of working with *women* in commercial sexual exploitation. This does NOT mean that we wish to ignore or exclude the many male and transgender people who sell sex, and who are victims of commercial sexual exploitation. We have chosen to do this simply for ease and clarity of expression. We hope that teams working with male and transgender victims will understand this and "translate" the language accordingly.

The book is designed to guide readers through a process of developing a ministry. It contains narratives which follow the progress of various characters in order to illustrate the didactic material. It can be read as a continuous whole, but it is also designed so that readers can dip in and out, choosing the topic which is most relevant for their training needs. Many of the stories we tell reflect the fact that the world of commercial sexual exploitation is one of violence and extreme suffering. We therefore recommend that you don't read the book late at night and that you balance your reading with activities which bring you life and joy.

It is our prayer that this book will be a blessing and inspiration to the many colleagues and friends throughout the world who are passionate about ending commercial sexual exploitation. It is our deep desire, hope and expectation that people involved in commercial sexual exploitation can "walk into freedom" – away from slavery, exploitation, violence, and addiction, into the "unforced rhythms of grace". As practitioners, we are called to accompany them on this journey, confident that we will be equipped for the task as we keep company with Jesus, learning together how to live "freely and lightly" with him. Lastly, we are dedicating this book to Carmel Mooney, who for many years has selflessly cared for the women on the streets of Luton. At 86 years old, Carmel is still operating as a frontline volunteer for Azalea in Luton, England. Carmel normalises inspirational care, and with her heart of radical love, "just gets on with it." We love you, Carmel!

Acknowledgements

WE ARE GRATEFUL to the many who have taught us over the years and so contributed indirectly to the writing of this book. We are thankful for Ken and Douglas, Lois, Tatiana and Angus who have faithfully walked with us and supported us throughout the journey. We are indebted to Ian Smith whose wonderful drawings have brought the text to life with humour and sensitivity. Thanks go to Dr Lauran Bethell, Dr Francesca Nuzzolese and members of ICAP for giving us international perspectives, experience and stories on which to draw, to Dr Angèle Carruthers who advised on medical matters, and to Geraldine Willford who proof-read the final text. Thanks also to the team at Azalea – staff, trustees and volunteers, who have contributed to the writing of this book both directly and indirectly. DAIP (Domestic Abuse Intervention Programs of Duluth, MN) kindly gave permission to adapt and use the image of the Power and Control Wheel. We are deeply grateful to Bob Ekblad for agreeing to include *Walk into Freedom* in his People's Seminary Press series.

Starting out in ministry

CHAPTER 1

Commercial Sexual Exploitation: The Basics

God created human beings; He created them godlike, reflecting God's nature. He created them male and female.

Genesis 1:27 (The Message)

1. Prostitution and commercial sexual exploitation

JODY WAS BROUGHT up in a children's home in the UK. She had been taken away from her mother, who was alcoholic and unable to look after her, at the age of six months. When she was sixteen she met Amir, who befriended her and took her out for coffee. He seemed so nice and she grew to trust him. When they slept together, he told her that he loved her. But things began to change. Amir introduced her to his friends, who gang raped her. After that he said she was a "slut" and made her work on the streets to earn money for him. Jody didn't like this, but Amir began to beat her if she didn't do as she was told, and gave her drugs to help her feel better.

Across the world, there are different stories to tell. Nell grew up in a small village in the mountains of Thailand, in a desperately poor family. Her father was an opium addict and her mother couldn't earn enough from working in the fields to care for her six children. So when Nell was ten, her mother sent her away to the city to work. Nell now sends the money she earns in the brothel back to her mother, to help feed the rest of the family. In India, Rani is a highly talented dancer and singer who uses these skills to entertain her customers and views her work in prostitution as her profession. She lives in a community with other women and considers herself superior to those women who only sell sexual favours. Rani knows that she will be beaten if she does not perform well and please her customers.

Jody, Nell and Rani are all working in prostitution. Many people believe that prostitution is no different from any other business transaction: a service is provided, and money is exchanged. But this understanding of prostitution assumes certain things: that the people offering the sexual services are doing so voluntarily, that they get to keep the money they earn, that they can work safely, that the people who buy their services treat them with respect. Over thirty years of experience of ministry among people caught up in prostitution has taught us that for the vast majority of people involved in it, the reality is quite different. It is true that there are some people who sell sexual services on their own terms, who are able to make their own decisions, and who would not consider themselves to be exploited in any way – for example, some "call girls" or gigolos. But these are very much in the minority. For the vast majority of those who work in it – the world of prostitution is highly dangerous and harmful. Many, if not most, of those who are caught up in prostitution are involved against their will, closely controlled by pimps or gangs, and deeply traumatised and damaged by their experiences. Jody is dependent on Amir to provide her with the drugs she needs to get through the day, and lives in fear of the next beating. It broke Nell's mother's heart to send her away but she felt she had no choice – but to the brothel manager and to her clients Nell was nothing more than an object. Rani knows that she cannot leave the community, even if she sometimes dreams of doing so, and knows that if she tried to leave, she would be tracked down and returned. It is because of the experience of Jody, Nell, Rani, and millions like them throughout the world who find that they are in a world of violence and enslavement that we believe prostitution to be exploitation.

2. The people and the work

Every Tuesday at 2pm, Jenny met with a man who insisted she call him "Uncle Andrew". They always met in the same place, under the tree by the bench. Jenny dreaded this weekly meeting, because "Uncle Andrew messed with her head." He bought her a school uniform. Jenny, who was 5' 2", was to wear it when they met, and she was to pretend to be Cindy – his 10 year-old niece – for one hour a week. Uncle Andrew would read her a story, and praise her for being a good girl. Her reward was to stroke his penis gently. If he climaxed, her reward was to do it again. If he didn't, he would slap her face with the story book. He always paid her well, and was very polite when he left, as if she was a "lady". As part of the deal, Jenny was to wave enthusiastically as Uncle Andrew drove away.

Uncle Andrew

People involved in commercial sexual exploitation work in various settings – in massage parlours, saunas, dance clubs and brothels, or on the streets. Some operate from private apartments, organising appointments by telephone or online. While some who work in prostitution are able to manage their own working arrangements, most often, they are under the control of someone else. Women who work in brothels or massage parlours may be managed by a "madam", and sometimes they have a contract and working agreement. Women who work on the streets, or in apartments, are often under the control of a pimp who "manages" the money that they earn. The pimp/perpetrator[1] may be a boyfriend or even a family member. On the surface, it will look like he is looking after her and protecting her. In reality, however, he is likely to be controlling her, giving her only a small amount of the earnings (if any at all) and threatening her with physical violence.

While it is mostly women who sell sex to male customers, male prostitution, in which men sell sex to other men, is also a lucrative business. Some women do pay for sexual services from men, but this is much rarer. Human sexuality is complex and the "sex industry", as it is often called, reflects this – it is far from straightforward. For example, some men want to buy sex from men who look like women, but who have not undergone a sex-change operation e.g. the "lady boys" of Thailand. Transgendered people also work in commercial sexual exploitation.

The women's working environments can be anything from plush clubs to filthy alleys, or even public parks, as in Jenny's case. Potential clients (often called "johns") may drive around the streets at night looking for women to pick up, visit brothels, or phone to make arrangements for appointments. Many more, however, find business through dedicated websites in which women advertise their services. Indeed, according to one British report, "Adult services websites are the most significant enabler of commercial sexual exploitation."[2] Photographs of the girls are displayed, descriptions of their physical attributes and services they offer are given, and "reviews" of previous clients are published. The site charges a fee to the individual placing the advert, but it is free for buyers to access the site. The buyer contacts the "seller" through a phone number provided on the site. What used to be called "escorting" is arranged by mobile phone. The sex-buyer makes contact and a place to meet is arranged. It is known that transactions conducted from the sex-buyer's homes can be particularly dangerous as the women have no security and no means of escape. Women who work in apartments or via mobile phones are far less visible and so much more difficult to reach than those who work on the streets or in clubs and brothels. They are also invisible to statutory care providers, "falling through the cracks" of welfare systems which may be available to help them to leave their current situations or to recover. Not all people involved in "selling sex" have actual

1. In the UK, practitioners often refer to pimps as "perpetrators".
2. https//appgprostituion.uk/enquiry/(accessed 6th July 2019).

contact with customers. Strippers, dancers, and those who offer "telephone sex" also provide some kind of sexual service to buyers, but without actual physical contact.

Pimps/perpetrators and managers cater for specific markets – foreign or underage girls might be offered, for example, or intercourse without the use of a condom. In many settings, the younger the girl, the more the client will pay. The "girlfriend" experience (GFE) is one in which kissing can be involved (usually the women do not want to do this – it is considered too intimate) and the woman stays overnight with the buyer. Some women specialise in sado-masochism or "dominatrix" services. In all of this, it is the woman's job to please the client, and to do whatever he wants, because he is paying. The client holds the power in the transaction, and the woman is there to please him. Jenny must do whatever "Uncle Andrew" wants, which could mean anything from listening to his troubles, to fulfilling his sexual fantasies, however "unusual" these might be.

It used to be thought that people go into commercial sexual exploitation because of mental illness (for example a sexual obsession or neurosis) or because of sinful desire. Thankfully, we know better now. The fact is that people become involved in commercial sexual exploitation because it is a way to make money, whether for themselves or (usually) someone else. A single mother, for example, might see commercial sexual exploitation as the only way to supplement her family's income. Some go "on the game" to pay for a drug habit, their own or another's, others to supplement welfare benefits or wages. Others may need to pay off debts. In Asia, as in Nell's case, many find that commercial sexual exploitation is the only option for a young woman to be able to support her family – particularly where there are few opportunities for education. In India, in some areas, commercial sexual exploitation is the family "business", and there is no option for a woman to work in anything else. Rani knows nothing else and is unlikely to think that any other way of life would be possible for her. Except in these particular settings, most women are likely to be separated from or estranged from their families – including their own children. We know this – routes into prostitution may vary throughout the world, but the experience of being a "nonperson" and the physical and sexual abuse by pimps and clients is the same everywhere.

Waving Uncle Andrew Goodbye

3. Brothels

Brothels are far more common than the general public might realise. Over a two-year period in Bristol, England, for example, police identified 65 operational brothels, over three-quarters of which had links to organised crime groups.[3] Brothels are to be found everywhere from social housing estates to luxury penthouses. Sometimes a whole building is owned by an "off-shore company" (i.e. private anonymous individuals or gangs who are difficult to trace) and used as a brothel. This means that no individual is named as responsible, and there are no neighbours in the building to complain. Some brothels are to be found in exclusive flats in affluent areas, again anonymously owned, making it difficult to trace who is making the money and controlling things. Massage parlours often masquerade as legitimate businesses, while in the background women are being transported to hotels and private addresses.

Brothels may offer particular services, advertising (for example) "All foreign girls" or the "Girlfriend Experience." Large sporting events provide pimps and traffickers with an opportunity to make more money: women are moved to where they know the clients will be, and the brothels, clubs and massage parlours see an increase in business. During the London Olympics in 2012, for example, police found that women were being moved to where clients would be, and that a number of exclusive "higher class" brothels were opened for the duration of the games.[4] A common model of operation used by organised crime groups engaged in commercial sexual exploitation involves setting up temporary, so-called "pop-op" brothels in residential properties. Online sites such as airbnb and Booking.com provide opportunities for pimps/perpetrators and madams to find short-term accommodation in which to operate. These can be hard for the police to control. As soon as one brothel is closed another will appear somewhere else – the women are moved from city to city and town to town, and given no choice in the

Moved on by the gang

---

3. Michael Skidmore, Sarah Garner, Ruth Crocker, Sarah Webb, John Graham and Martin Gill *The Role and Impact of Organised Crime in the Local Off-Street Sex Market* The Police Foundation & Perpetuity Research 2016.

4. https://i3.cmsfiles.com/eaves/2013/06/Capital-Exploits-June-2013.pdf-da8819.pdf (accessed 6th July 2019)

matter. This avoids police detection and at the same time maintains control over the women, causing great uncertainty and fear in their lives. Most of these women are not known to the statutory services and so do not have access to care and help to leave commercial sexual exploitation should they wish to do so.

4. Sex trafficking

It is important to make a distinction between commercial sexual exploitation and sex trafficking. Human trafficking is defined by the United Nations as,

> the recruitment, transportation, transfer, harbouring or receipt of persons, by means of the threat or use of force or other forms of coercion, of abduction, of fraud, of deception, of the abuse of power or of a position of vulnerability or of the giving or receiving of payments or benefits to achieve the consent of a person having control over another person, for the purpose of exploitation. Exploitation shall include at a minimum, the exploitation of the prostitution of others or other forms of sexual exploitation, forced labour or services, slavery or practices similar to slavery, servitude or the removal of organs.[5]

The term "human trafficking", therefore, can refer to many different types of slavery, such as domestic servitude or bonded labour in a factory or mine. Coercion to work in the "sex industry" is only one aspect of human trafficking. People who are trafficked for the purposes of prostitution may have trusted an individual who has promised them a legitimate job perhaps in another country. Many are tricked into paying for travel to different countries. Maria was in her fifties when she was promised a job (by a family member) in Europe as a cleaner. Thinking that she would be able to work hard for a while and send back money to Nigeria in order to pay for her son's education and her ageing parents' health care, she readily accepted the offer. When she arrived in Switzerland, she was met at the airport and taken to an apartment where she was kept for several days. Eventually, she was told that the cleaning job had fallen through and that she would have to work in a brothel. She said she wanted to go home, but was told she would have to work in order to pay for her ticket. Maria's story ended happily. She managed to escape and was helped by a charity to get back home. Not everyone is quite so fortunate.

Criminal gangs use personal contact and the internet to trick and lure women into danger. They target children's homes, schools, and homeless shelters, shopping malls and dance venues. The supply of vulnerable people is limitless, and the exploiters know exactly how to lure them in. In her book *Walking Prey*, Holly Austin Smith writes of how easy and how prevalent it is in the United States for vulnerable teenage girls to be lured into commercial sexual exploitation by

---

5. Article 3, paragraph (a) of The United Nations Protocol to Prevent, Suppress and Punish Trafficking in Persons.

traffickers and sex buyers.[6] In the UK recently, there have been several instances of gangs targeting vulnerable young girls who live in children's homes, and forcing them to work in prostitution.[7] In the Netherlands, young men who groom young girls are known as "loverboys". Jody's story illustrates how groomers work. The man finds a vulnerable young girl and pretends to be her boyfriend, telling her how special she is. He buys her clothes and presents and then introduces her to sex with other men. Soon, however, he will say that they have run out of money, and suggest that since she has slept with so many men it will be easy for her to make money by selling sex. So begins her life of commercial sexual exploitation. Since these activities do not necessarily involve overseas travel, they may be classed as "internal trafficking".

People who are displaced because of war or persecution, or who are attempting to move away from desperate economic situations, are at high risk of being trafficked. Women from areas of desperate poverty are vulnerable to being trafficked by criminal gangs, lured abroad to find employment perhaps to support families at home or simply to find a better way of life. For example, many women are trafficked from Eastern Europe to Western Europe, from Nigeria to the Middle East and Europe, from Russia to Israel, from the rural areas of Asia to the cities.[8] These women find themselves working in brothels, dance clubs or massage parlours or apartments, kept under the control of their pimps. In England in 2017, it was found that highly organised gangs were trafficking women from China, Hong Kong and South Korea into England and moving them to different locations and exploiting them in hotel rooms. This led major hotel groups, such as Hilton and Shiva, to train their staff to be able to spot and report signs of trafficking, and raise awareness of the issue amongst their guests.[9] Sex trafficking is changing the face of commercial sexual exploitation in western cities. For example, it used to be thought that the women who worked on the streets of London and those who worked "off street" in clubs and brothels were two entirely separate groups. However, it is now recognised that the lines between these groups are becoming increasingly blurred as traffickers move women around among various locations and settings.[10]

6. Holly Austin Smith *Walking Prey: How America's Youth are Vulnerable to Sex Slavery* NY: St Martin's Press 2104.

7. See for example, Andrew Norfolk's report in *The Times* newspaper Wednesday January 5th 2011, on the scandal in Rotherham, England https://www.thetimes.co.uk/article/revealed-conspiracy-of-silence-on-uk-sex-gangs-gpg5vqsqz9h (accessed 13th July 2020).

8. For the most up to date knowledge of the global trafficking situation, see the annual Trafficking in Persons Report which is produced by the US State Department. https://www.state.gov/trafficking-in-persons-report/

9. https://www.unhcr.org/uk/staistics/unhcrstats/5d08d7ee7/unhcr-global-trands-2018.html (accessed 6th July, 2019)

10. Julie Bindel, Ruth Beslin and Laura Brown *Capital Exploits: A Study of Prostitution and Trafficking in London* Eaves Report 2013, 33.

The growth in human trafficking in recent years has been fuelled by the lure of profit, and the low risk of being caught. It is also caused by desperate poverty, and marketing which persuades people that they need to have an affluent lifestyle in order to be happy. The trafficking of women and girls for the purposes of sexual exploitation is a highly lucrative branch of organised crime, comparable to weapons and drugs. Unlike drugs, however, this human commodity can be sold over and over again. And the commodity is expendable. If and when women become unwell from ill treatment or disease, they are considered to be of no use and may be killed. There are always many others who can take their place to make money for the gangs who control them. In many countries, if a woman manages to escape she is unlikely to go to the police because of corruption. There is always a risk of being sold back to the traffickers or of being sexually exploited once more by the police themselves.

The lover boy

5. Summing Up

Not everyone shares our view that prostitution is sexual exploitation. There are very active groups who argue that prostitution should be considered a job like any other.[11] However, while we recognise that some women are able to work in the sex industry and maintain their independence, we believe that the vast majority of people who become involved in prostitution are being exploited not only by their pimps and "managers" but by their clients, and subject to coercion and the threat of violence. These women are treated as objects rather than human beings. Speaking in Stockholm in 2002, Gunilla Ekberg pulled no punches as she described the reality of commercial sexual exploitation:

> "In prostitution, men use women's and girls' bodies, vaginas, anuses, mouths for their sexual pleasures and as vessels of ejaculation, over and over and over again. Prostitution is not sexual liberation; it is humiliation, it is torture, it is

---

11. See for example COYOTE RI http://coyoteri.org/wp/ (accessed 12/07/20)

rape, it is sexual exploitation and should be named as such. Consequently, males who use women and girls in prostitution are sexual predators and rapists."[12]

Ekberg's words underline the fact that women in commercial sexual exploitation are looked on as objects to be used and thrown away when they are no longer needed – useful only for making money or sexual gratification. However, in God's eyes they are not objects but made in his image, prized and precious. It is people like Jody, Nell, Rani and Jenny to whom we want to reach out, giving them opportunities for freedom, to become the people they want to be and to find new life in Christ.

BIBLE STUDY

Read Genesis 1:26-31
This is the story of how God created men and women. Without exception, all men and women were created in God's image – they share God's characteristics. They were given responsibility and dignity, and all that they needed for nourishment and beauty. The equality of which this passage speaks applies to the relationships between men and women, and between all human beings. No one is superior to any one else in God's eyes. Everyone has intrinsic value and worth, deserving of respect. This is why the kind of objectification that we see in commercial sexual exploitation is so wrong. It violates everything that God intended for his people. No-one is an object to be used.

QUESTIONS FOR DISCUSSION

> What does it mean to say that all men and women are made in the image of God?
> In what ways does commercial exploitation violate God's view of humanity?
> What does prostitution/ commercial sexual exploitation look like in your setting?
> What are the cultural and religious attitudes towards prostitution in your setting?
> What are the principal forms of human trafficking in your setting?
> What do you think of Jenny's story? Why do you think she said that Uncle Andrew "messed with her head"? What is wrong with Uncle Andrew's behaviour?

---

12. Gunilla Ekberg, Special Advisor on issues of prostitution and trafficking in women at the Swedish Division for Gender Equality, at the Nov. 2002 Seminar on the Effects of Legalisation of Prostitution Activities in Stockholm https://prostitution.procon.org/view.answers.php?question-ID=000102 (accessed 12/07/20)

CHAPTER 2

The Bigger Picture

"Whoever oppresses the poor shows contempt for their Maker, but whoever is kind to the needy honours God."

Proverbs 14:31

"We, the survivors of prostitution and trafficking gathered at this press conference today, declare that prostitution is violence against women. Women in prostitution do not wake up one day and "choose" to be prostitutes. It is chosen for us by poverty, past sexual abuse, the pimps who take advantage of our vulnerabilities, and the men who buy us for the sex of prostitution."

Manifesto of survivors of prostitution and trafficking press conference, European Parliament, 17th October 2005.

1. Prostitution – more than meets the eye

THE MEETING WAS to start at 7pm, and we were looking forward to sharing how we were going to tackle the problem of commercial sexual exploitation in the area. But our enthusiasm was not matched by the local population, for only one person, a man, turned up. Undaunted, Philippa started to go through her prepared presentation. She explained that all the women on the streets came from backgrounds of abuse and exploitation, and that they were very vulnerable. However, before she could go any further, the man blurted out, "I really can't agree with what you are saying! I cannot agree with you that these women are vulnerable. I see them every day in my street and they are NOT weak women. They are strong, clever women who know exactly what they are doing! I agree that they are vulnerable in that they look terribly ill, but the reason they look ill is that they are all on drugs. They are out there because of their addiction. They are NOT out there because they are being exploited. If anything, they are exploiting us! They approach you for sex, telling you what they will do for a fiver. It's disgusting!"

We don't want them here

We soon learned that the man – we'll call him Michael – had come to the meeting in the hope that we would be able to pressurise the police into doing something about the problem of the women who were working in his area. His concerns were legitimate – it is well known that street prostitution is associated with drug dealing and violence. Local residents feel threatened and women in particular often feel they cannot walk safely without being approached by would-be sex buyers. Crime levels tend to be higher, and used condoms and needles left lying on the streets pose a threat to public health. Property values reduce as the crime rates rise – no wonder local residents get angry.

For Michael, as for many people, the way to tackle the problem was to target the women, stopping them soliciting on the streets and punishing them for their anti-social behaviour. But is this the best approach to take? In order to understand the nature of commercial exploitation, and to think through ways to tackle it, we need to be able to see the bigger picture. We need to look beyond what is immediately obvious and ask some important but difficult questions. What are the causes of prostitution? Why is the "sex industry" such big business? How is prostitution viewed by the law?

2. The bigger picture

In the last chapter we saw that most women who are working in prostitution are there because they, or someone else, needs the money. For the vast majority throughout the world, the reason is poverty. Many factors contribute to women's poverty – gender inequality, racism, economic and political instability, amongst other things, all contribute to women becoming caught up in commercial sexual exploitation. For example, Diya had to find work in the bars of Calcutta because she had been abandoned as a child. There were already four daughters in the family and her father said he couldn't afford to pay for five dowries, so Diya had to go, giving up her dreams of getting an education and a good job. Aisah managed to get away from her village in Malaysia and thought she had got a good job as a servant in a big house in the city,

The Bigger Picture

but she was soon made to sleep with the house-owner's "friends". She was told that if she did not do so, she would never see her family again.

Wherever there is a view that women are inferior, or that certain groups of human beings are superior to others, women and girls will be exploited. When there is political upheaval or instability, and little scope for employment or education, women and girls will be exploited. Another cause of commercial sexual exploitation is human greed – there are huge profits to be made, and the pimps/perpetrators and gangsters will do anything to get their hands on the money. And lastly, a primary root cause of prostitution is that there is a market for it: put simply, men want to buy sex. One senior policeman put it this way:

Diya had to go

> "How will the traffickers survive without sex buyers? The sex buyers are the crucial sponsors of organised crime. The traffickers are not in this because of sex….They are in this because of money." [13]

Exactly the same might be said of pimps, madams, and brothel owners. If there were no demand, there would be no supply. But, unfortunately, there are millions of men on the planet who do buy sex, and for as long as this is the case, prostitution and commercial sexual exploitation will not go away.

3. Prostitution and the law

At present, there are different opinions throughout the world as to how to deal with commercial sexual exploitation. In some countries, such as Greece and Indonesia, prostitution (including pimping and running a brothel) is entirely legal. In others, such as China and Egypt, prostitution is banned. In the UK it is illegal to run a brothel but not for an individual to sell sexual services. In America and Australia, the situation varies across various states: some have decriminalised sex work (in other words, they do not prosecute those involved in prostitution) while others have legalised it, meaning that women in prostitution are considered to have a job like any other, that they are subject to employment law, and pay tax. However, efforts

---

13. Detective Inspector Simon Haggstrom, head of Stockholm Police Prostitution Unit. Quoted in Banyard, K. *Pimp State: Sex, Money and the Future of Equality*, London: Faber and Faber, 2016, 196.

to legalise it (for example, the Netherlands and Germany) have not been successful in breaking the link between criminality and prostitution, with many legal brothels and clubs being used as fronts for sex trafficking and money laundering.

In many countries today, it is recognised that the people who control the women – pimps, madams and so forth – deserve to be punished. For much of history, however, the commonly held view has been that if prostitution is to be curbed, then the women, as well as the pimps and madams, should be penalized. Consequently, women have been arrested, put in prison, made to work in laundries and factories, medicated to curb their sexual instincts, and fined. However, the wisdom and efficacy of punishing women who work in prostitution is increasingly being questioned. First, when we target the women, we are making the assumption that they are always free agents able to make their own choices. However, most women working in prostitution do so because they do not have alternative ways of making a living – because of poverty, lack of education, lack of opportunities, addiction, or because they have been coerced or duped by others. Moreover, very few women are not under the control of a pimp/perpetrator or manager, and if they are not when they start out, they soon will be. There is so much money to be made from prostitution that pimps and gangsters do not hesitate to resort to violence to make sure that their source of income is kept under their control. Should we really be punishing women who are enslaved in this way?

Second, this approach doesn't do the women themselves any good. If they are fined, the only way they can pay these fines is to sell sex – so they are caught in a vicious circle. If they go to prison, they may be able to stop taking drugs for a while (if that has been an issue), but the likelihood is that they will be targeted when they come out and lured or forced back into their old life. In fact, the chances are that this is the only life they know, and that as soon as they are released they will go back to what is familiar. Third, the fact that they have been in prostitution means that they are likely to have had almost no education or training, which makes it very difficult to get a job. Prostitution is all that they know – a fact which pimps and perpetrators and can use to control the women, preventing them from leaving. How are they going to learn new skills? Not only that, if they have a criminal conviction they will find it much harder, if not impossible, to find alternative employment.

For all these reasons, some western countries (e.g. Sweden, Iceland, and Ireland) have adopted the "Nordic model" in which buyers rather than sellers of sex are punished. This approach takes the view that to penalise women in prostitution is to penalise those who are already vulnerable and exploited.[14]

14. For information on and discussion of the "Nordic Model" see May-Len Skilbrei & Charlotta Holmström *Prostitution Policy in the Nordic Region: Ambiguous Sympathies* New York: Routledge 2016

4. Demand: Why do men purchase sex?

Many countries are reviewing the law regarding prostitution as the realisation increases that most of the women involved are being exploited rather than themselves exploiting others. But another aspect of knowing the "bigger picture" of commercial sexual exploitation is a need to understand who their customers are and why they want to use women in prostitution in the first place.

Of course, this also varies throughout the world. According to recent surveys carried out in European cities, men who buy sex tend to be educated, middle-income professionals, aged between 25 and 34 years. Many are married or in a relationship, and often they will look for a sex worker during the day or before or after work. [15] The red-light areas of European cities are magnets for young men out for adventure and fun. Visiting a brothel, booking an "escort", or looking for a woman on the streets is often a clandestine activity, perhaps made more thrilling because of the risk of being found out.

In some Asian cultures, on the other hand, a visit to a brothel is part of an evening's entertainment, part of a "good night out with friends".[16] It is not uncommon for the offer of a visit to a brothel to be included in corporate hospitality packages for business men. In so-called "sex tourism" many men travel thousands of miles to access "exotic" women and underage girls.

But why do such men want to pay for sex? For some, it is the thrill of variety or the desire for sexual experience without the obligation of a relationship. It is also known that some go to prostitutes because of loneliness, seeking emotional comfort as well as sexual fulfilment.[17] For many, however, the use of a woman in prostitution is a matter of power, of being in control: paying for the use of another's body for a while means that the sex buyer can do whatever he wants with that body for the duration of the encounter. Some interesting quotes from those who took part in the Eaves report on sex buyers reveal the attitudes of many of the men: "We're living in the age of instant coffee, instant food. This is instant sex"; "Prostitution is being able to do what you want without the taxation"; "It's a financial transaction." The idea that women should be "available", whether online or as corporate entertainment, carries at its heart a belief that women are objects and that men have a right to satisfy their sexual desires in whatever way they wish. Some sex buyers can and do convince themselves that they are helping the women. For, example,

---

15. See, for example, Richard Layte et al. (2006). *The Irish Study of Sexual Health and Relationships* Dublin: Crisis Pregnancy Agency and Department of Health and Children in which 7,441 adults were interviewed.

16. Kevin Bales *Disposable People: New Slavery in the Global Economy* (rev ed) Berkeley: University of California Press 2000, 45.

17. Melissa Farley, Julie Bindell & Jacqueline M Golding *Men Who Buy Sex: Who They Buy and What they Know* London: Eaves 2009. https://i1.cmsfiles.com/eaves/2012/04/MenWhoBuySex-89396b.pdf accessed 11th July 2019.

many sex tourists travel to countries such as the Dominican Republic or Thailand for the sole purpose of buying sex, seeing their "custom" as helping the women to make money and support their families.[18] In reality, however, they are merely using the women for their own gratification. Online communities exist in which men discuss and compare their experiences with women, and make recommendations to others, in the same way that people discuss purchasing cars or washing machines. For them, buying sex is no different to buying any other commodity.[19]

So what can change the situation? Would it make a difference if sex buyers knew that most women and girls are exploited? While sex buyers might like to think that the women are fully consenting adults, they are unlikely to make enquiries as to whether or not that is the case. The reality is that most men who use women in prostitution are not interested in who the women are as human beings but simply see them as objects to be used. As Julie Currie, an officer in the London Metropolitan police Modern Slavery and Kidnap Unit says, "In the vast majority of cases males paying for sex will give no thought to where the woman has come from or what circumstances have led her into prostitution."[20]

Would a change in the law act as a deterrent? Some studies have suggested that placing buyers on a register of sex offenders would make them think again. Some men have said that the threat of a prison sentence would do this, or public exposure in a "naming and shaming" exercise – for example, letters to their family or employer. This will not work, of course, amongst men who have no family or reputation to lose, or whose culture dictates that to use women in prostitution is simply to exercise their rights as males.

It is good that there is a growing realisation of the role of sex buyers in commercial sexual exploitation. However, there is also a risk that sex buyers become demonised in the way that women historically have been. This would be to polarise the situation in an unhealthy way, for nothing is ever straightforward in this life, and we need to avoid "black and white" thinking. Just as there are complex reasons for women becoming commercially sexually exploited, so there are many factors which contribute to the huge demand for their services. It is known that loneliness is a major cause in many cases. Some men may feel a sense of inadequacy or find it difficult to maintain healthy relationships with women. A major factor is our hypersexualised

---

18. See Denise Brennan *What's Love Got to Do With It? Transnational Desires and Sex Tourism in the Dominican Republic* Durham: Duke University Press 2004.

19. Coy, M., Horvath, M., and Kelly, L. (2007) "'It's just like going to the supermarket': Men buying sex in East London" London: Child and Woman Abuse Studies Unit London Metropolitan University

20. https://appgprostitution.uk/wp-content/uploads/2018/05/Behind-closed-doors-APPG-on-Prostitution.pdf (accessed 12/07/20) "Behind Closed Doors: Organised Sexual Exploitation in England and Wales: An Enquiry by the All Party Parliamentary Group on Prostitution and the Global Sex Trade" 2018, 3.

culture in which sex is used to sell everything from DIY tools to food. The idea that sex is our right and an entitlement is constant in many societies, as is the idea that we should be able to have sex wherever and with whomever we want. The ready availability of pornography serves to underscore this view. It is reckoned that 64% of teenagers (13-24 year olds) watch pornography regularly, and that 3-5% of Americans are addicted to sex.[21] Both men and women use pornography, but it is known that many men who do so also visit women in prostitution. The porn industry insidiously influences and encourages the idea that men may do whatever they want with women, and that women are there merely to please them. In other words, the porn industry contributes to the idea that women are objects rather than human beings.

You feel quite empty

Up till now we might be forgiven for thinking that it is only the women who are harmed in commercial sexual exploitation. However, hidden away among the quotes given by sex buyers in the Eaves research is another which tells a different story: "It's unfulfilling, there's no reward", says one man. "It's empty. It's terrible. You come out feeling even more empty and unloved. You will likely feel quite empty afterwards, as if you have been used." This suggests that what began as an exciting, anonymous sexual encounter has left only shame and emptiness. Jay Stringer, who has researched into male sex addiction, speaks of desires being "hijacked" when men repeatedly buy sex. Listening to men who had gone to South Korea as "sex tourists", he heard story after story of men who had come to hate what they were involved in. He writes,

> "Each man spoke of seeing a deadness in the eyes of the women and teenagers that they had purchased sex from. One particularly honest man told me he went to a small village in Thailand where he was treated like a king. He was given access to any woman or child he desired. He put it like this: "I remember

---

21. Teens using porn – see "18 shocking stats about the Porn Industry and its Underage Consumers" Fight the New Drug September 5, 2017 https:// fight thenewdrug.org/10-porn-stats-that-will-blow-your-mind/. For sex addition – see Stacy Notaras Murphy "It's not about Sex" Counselling Today December 1 2011 http://ct.counselling.org/2011/12/its-not-about-sex/. Both of these are referred to in Jay Stringer *Unwanted: How Sexual Brokenness Reveals our way to Healing* Carol Stream: NavPress 2018, Kindle Location 369.

thinking, who have I become? It started with a fantasy about having sex in Thailand, and by the end of my trip I was doing horrible things I swore I would never do in my life."[22]

These testimonies tell of men who had become caught up in behaviour which led only to emptiness and shame. Many, however, find it difficult to break out of a cycle of pleasure and thrill seeking. What begins as "harmless" fun ends up as an addiction which becomes stronger than the individual. Stringer says that as he conducted his research he became increasingly aware that

> "our battle is not solely against the flesh and blood of personal sexual brokenness but against the powers and principalities of this world that delight in seeing God's gift of sex debased."[23]

Commercial sexual exploitation is harmful for everyone concerned – including those who profit from it. They, too, are often caught up in webs of violent criminality much bigger than themselves, from which they, too, can find it nigh on impossible to escape. When men and women come to view other human beings as objects, or to view sexual activity as divorced from relationship and responsibility, when they become addicted to or embroiled in patterns of behaviour which can damage them physically and mentally and destroy relationships and families – their dignity as people made in the image of God is compromised, God's creation is marred, and a great deal of suffering is caused.

5. Beginning to think things through

In this chapter, we have tried to explain just how complicated the causes of commercial exploitation are. It's good to be able to report that Michael left that evening with a greater understanding of what was going on around him and a willingness to join us in our effort to work against the exploitation of women. He was right to say that the women are clever and strong, but he hadn't realised that they have to be that way in order to survive. He hadn't realised that their aggression was borne out of fear and desperation – and why should he? He didn't know that most of them would be controlled by pimps who were most likely also supplying them with the drugs they needed the money to buy. And it hadn't dawned on him that the women wouldn't have been there at all if there were no customers around.

But all this is not to say that the people caught up in it are without personal responsibility: to understand the reasons for someone's behaviour is not to excuse or justify it, or absolve the person of personal responsibility. However, the more we can see beyond what is immediately in front of us, the more we see the bigger

---

22. Stringer *Unwanted* Kindle Location 2201
23. Stringer *Unwanted* Kindle Location 2212

picture, the better we will be able to work to bring effective and lasting change in peoples' lives.

BIBLE STUDY

Read the story of Rahab in Joshua 2:1-24

Prostitution would not exist if there were no demand for purchasing sex. Rahab set up her brothel on the edge of the city where travellers, military people and so forth would be likely to be able to find her. In this way she was able to support her family, in an age when most women were completely dependent on men. The spies sent out by Joshua made a bee-line for the local brothel when they reached the town, and Rahab showed herself to be not only an astute business woman, she also made sure that her family was safe when the country was invaded. This clever woman, despite the fact that she is ostracised by mainstream society, plays her part in God's plan for Israel, and despite the fact that she works in prostitution she is an ancestor to Jesus himself and honoured as a woman of faith.

QUESTIONS FOR DISCUSSION

> In many cultures, women in prostitution are seen as the "lowest of the low", ostracised and stigmatised by mainstream society. However, the story of Rahab shows her to be shrewd and clever. Not only that she is recorded as being an ancestress of Jesus. How does this affect your thinking about women in prostitution?
> What is the legal situation regarding prostitution in your setting? What is your understanding of the "Nordic" approach and what do you think of it?
> Why is it wrong to treat people as objects?
> What can your Christian community do to work against the poverty which forces so many into commercial sexual exploitation?
> What are the implications of the idea that pimps, madams and sex buyers are made in the image of God?
> How would you help someone like Michael to see the bigger picture with regard to commercial sexual exploitation?

CHAPTER 3

What does the Bible have to say?

"Is not this the kind of fasting I have chosen: to loose the chains of injustice and untie the cords of the yoke, to set the oppressed free and break every yoke?"

Isaiah 58:6

1. Introduction

AS LYDIA READ her Bible and learned more about God's love for the fallen world, she felt she had to do something to help the women she saw every day on the streets of her city. For her it was straightforward: God commands us to work against injustice, and reach out to those who are rejected and hurting – including women in commercial sexual exploitation. So Lydia started going on outreach with some friends, and began to build up relationships with the women in the local brothels. She was always aware of God's presence with her as she went into the red-light area, even though she knew that she was being watched by the pimps who hung around on the street corners. Slowly, the women began to trust her and then one day, one of them came to her church. Lydia was delighted. What a breakthrough! But she was shocked to discover that Pastor Joe was not so happy. "You must not bring these women here," he said angrily. "The Bible says that women like these are impure sinners who should not be allowed in the sanctuary.

Pastor Joe

They must leave their sinful way of life and then they can come to church!" Lydia was devastated. Surely no one should be excluded from church? But Pastor Joe would have none of it – so long as "these women" were working in prostitution they had no place in God's house.

Lydia's belief that no one should be excluded from the church came from her understanding of God's love and mercy for everyone, and it came as a shock to discover that not everyone thought the way she did. Her experience shows how important it is to gain a theological perspective as part of the preparation for reaching out to the victims of commercial sexual exploitation. Our theological understanding will have a bearing on important questions such as whether prostitution should be legalised or not, or whether we should support the criminalisation of sex buyers. But it is also important with regard to our attitude towards the women with whom we work, because our unconscious assumptions and attitudes can affect the way we relate to people. Our cultures, experiences and church traditions all influence the development of our beliefs and prejudices. In this chapter we will look at what the Bible has to say about prostitution and commercial sexual exploitation – the causes, the women who engage in it, and the men who buy their services.

2. Tackling the causes – a Biblical View

We have seen that poverty, injustice and inequality all contribute to the existence of commercial sexual exploitation. In Biblical terms, these things are the result of humanity's broken relationship with God – in other words, human sin. Paul explains this in chapters 1-3 of his letter to the Romans. When men and women turned away from God, they became idolatrous, worshipping all sorts of created things rather than God (Rom 1:25). As a result, natural desires became distorted. The greed and desire for power over others which cause poverty, injustice and inequality are the result of humanity's broken relationship with God.

But Paul does not allow us to blame others for this situation, or to think that sin and idolatry are things that are "out there" and nothing to do with us. He insists that we all bear responsibility, for we all have been given a knowledge of right and wrong. We are all sinners who have fallen short of the glory of God. In other words, no one is the person God intended them to be. No one is righteous, he says, not even one! Paul then goes on to explain that it is only through Christ that we can be justified – "made righteous before God", and only as his disciples that we can begin to change and grow.

This means that when tackling injustice and exploitation we should start with ourselves. We have to recognise and deal with our own greed, lust and desire for power over others – bringing all these things under God's rule. Christians need to ask: Are we seeking power and status for ourselves? Are we promoting gender inequality in our churches? Are we indirectly contributing to the exploitation of others because of the things we buy? A major cause of commercial sexual exploitation is poverty, but as Bishop Zac Niringiye insists, we cannot tackle poverty without first tackling our own greed. In the same way, cannot tackle injustice and inequality in the world without looking at our own actions and behaviour towards others.

But the Bible is also clear that Christians should not be complacent and inward looking, wrapped up in our own concerns, ignoring the suffering and injustice which is all around us. The Old Testament prophets repeatedly call out for God's people to be involved in standing up for the oppressed, fighting injustice and bringing God's mercy to the poor. They object when they see people becoming more wrapped up in comfortable religiosity when there is injustice and oppression all around them (Amos 5:11-24; Hosea 6:6; Micah 6:1-6). Jesus takes the same view. When he is criticised for keeping company with tax collectors and sinners he says, "….go and learn what this means: 'I desire mercy, not sacrifice. For I have not come to call the righteous, but sinners" (Matthew 9:13). His command to his disciples at the end of Matthew's gospel is that they are to go out and make disciples of all nations (Matthew 28:19-20). Christians have a responsibility to take the message of God's love in to all areas of the world. That includes the dark and dangerous world of commercial sexual exploitation and all who are caught up in it – women, pimps/perpetrators, madams and buyers alike.

3. Prostitution – what the Bible has to say

Although Pastor Joe's reaction might seem extreme, his attitude reflects a view held amongst many Christians to varying degrees – that women who are involved in commercial sexual exploitation are somehow unclean and shameful. It is sad to say that many women who are or have been involved in prostitution find it difficult to be accepted by churches, and some find that they are rejected altogether. In large part this is because in some cultures the subject of prostitution is considered to be so shameful that it is simply not talked about, and the women involved are shunned or hidden away. However, it is also true that there are passages in Scripture which could be used to support this point of view. For example, in Leviticus 21:7,14 priests are forbidden from marrying anyone who is not a virgin – women working in prostitution, divorcees and widows. In Leviticus 21:9, it is stated that if a priest's daughter works in prostitution she must be put to death. These laws show that ideas of holiness and sexual purity were closely linked in ancient Israel. A priest had to ensure that they were always pure in order to work in the sanctuary, and his family had to be pure too. Any money made from prostitution could not be used for the upkeep of the sanctuary (Deuteronomy 23:18). But the laws about prostitution did not only refer to priests. Leviticus 19:29 says that men in general should not make their daughters work in prostitution. Since men had complete control over the women and girls in their families, prostitution could have been a very lucrative option for a poor family. However, the law is clear – to do this would degrade the girl and to bring something into society which is harmful for everyone. Interestingly, however, there is no prohibition against women working in prostitution or against men making use of their services. No woman should have had to resort to prostitution, for they should have been looked after by the men. However, widowhood or divorce meant that some women had to fend for themselves, and for some, prostitution might have been the only option.

Other passages provide evidence that women in prostitution were thought to be unclean. The prophets often use the idea of prostitution as a metaphor for idolatry. This can refer to chasing after other gods (e.g. Exodus 34:15-16), or simply doing what we want, rather than what God wants (e.g. Isaiah 23:15-17). The books of Hosea and Jeremiah use the metaphor of prostitution to warn against worshipping pagan gods. In the book of Ezekiel (chapters 16 and 23), Israel is likened to a woman who has become so depraved and degraded by her work in prostitution that she even sacrifices her own children. With disturbing and sometimes very crude language, Ezekiel uses the ideas of prostitution and sexual depravity as metaphors for unfaithfulness to God, and warns of harsh punishment if the leaders in Jerusalem do not mend their ways. This is in sharp contrast to the idea of marriage which is used to symbolise the kind of intimate relationship God wants to have with Israel. In all these books, the metaphor of the prostitute is used to warn people in power to remain faithful to God's covenant and to ensure justice for the people. We find a similar use of language in the Book of Revelation in the New Testament. The whore of Babylon is depicted as sitting on a scarlet beast which has seven heads and ten horns. She is said to be "Babylon the Great, the mother of whores and of earth's abominations" (Revelation 17:5 NRSV). She is a dreadful figure, associated with bloodshed and corruption, and she is eventually destroyed.

If we only had these texts, we might think that the message of the Bible is that women caught up in commercial sexual exploitation are the worst of sinners and deserve severe punishment. We might think that Pastor Joe is right – women in prostitution should not be welcome in our churches, and we should not be trying to reach out to them at all, but leave them to God's judgement. However, these are not the only voices on the matter in Scripture.

Within the Old Testament itself two stories give quite a different message. In Genesis 38, Tamar, the daughter-in-law of Judah is left a widow. According to law and custom, a widowed, childless woman should have been able to sleep with her dead husband's brother, in order for the family line to continue. However, the family does not fulfil its duty in this regard and Tamar is left with the prospect of remaining childless. So Tamar decides to take matters into her own hands. When Judah goes to Timnah for sheep shearing, Tamar sits at the side of the road, hiding her face with a veil. Judah sees her and propositions her, not knowing who she is. He has no money, but gives her his seal, cord and staff as a guarantee. They sleep together, and Tamar becomes pregnant. When this is discovered, the other women in the household denounce her as having "played the whore", and for this, Judah pronounces that she must be put to death. But Tamar still has the cord, seal and staff and announces that the father of the child is their owner. Judah, realising he has been duped, says that Tamar is more righteous than he is – she has ensured the continuation of the family line, which he had his family had not even tried to do. Tamar gives birth to twins, one of whom becomes the ancestor of King David.

Tamar and Rahab

In a second story, a Canaanite woman named Rahab owns a brothel (Joshua 2). Israelite spies sent to Canaan go straight there when they enter the land. Defying the king's demand that she hand them over to him, Rahab hides them in the roof of her house, telling them that the Canaanites are afraid of Israel because they know that God is with them. Rahab gains assurance from the men that her family will be safe and helps the men to escape. Because of her actions, Israel is able to conquer Canaan and settle there.

These two stories give us further insights into the way women in prostitution were viewed in ancient Israel, and there is a lot that is similar to today. Tamar worked at the side of the road, and Rahab's brothel was on the edge of town, well away from respectable society. Tamar's pregnancy was considered to have brought shame upon Judah's house – while no questions are asked about the father of the child. Despite the fact that Rahab facilitates the conquest of Canaan, she is always known as working in prostitution, and never shakes the label off. There were double standards then, just as there are today.

In ancient Israel, as in many societies today, women in general were considered to be morally, intellectually and physically inferior to men, and women working in prostitution were the lowest of the low. These stories, however, make fun of these assumptions and teach something quite different. In both, men are shown up as stupid, while the women are very clever indeed. The Israelite spies, instead of getting on with spying, head straight for a brothel, and are so indiscreet about it that the king immediately knows where to find them! Rahab, on the other hand, is the one who knows what God is doing. In the story of Tamar, Judah eventually has to admit that Tamar is more righteous than he is: she has ensured the continuation of the family line, which he and his sons had failed to do. These women not only get the better of the men, but ensure that God's will is done in the process! In the New Testament they are both included in Jesus' family tree. They are both ancestors of David and therefore of Jesus himself. They may have been deemed dishonourable by society, but God's view is different. In fact, Rahab is mentioned twice more in the New Testament, both times with honour (Hebrews 11:31 and James 2:25) – her involvement in prostitution does not exclude her from being called a woman of faith.

In the gospels, remarkably little is said about prostitution. A long-held tradition teaches that Mary Magdalene worked in prostitution, but there is actually no evidence for this. The same is often said of the woman who anoints Jesus' feet, mainly because she is described as a "sinner" in Luke's version of the story (Luke 7:36-50). But the word "sinner" need not imply this; if the woman had been working in prostitution, the gospel writers would surely have said so. In Matthew 21:31-32, Jesus tells the story of a man who had two sons. The first son is asked to go and work in the vineyard. At first, he refuses but then changes his mind. The second son says he will go, but does not. Clearly, it is the first son, despite his initial disobedience, who does what his father wants, while the second is being dishonest and hypocritical. There is a warning here – people who like to be seen to be religious and say all the right things need to watch out. For sometimes, those who appear to be obedient turn out not to be so, and those who seem to be rebelling – women working in prostitution and tax collectors, for example – turn out to be the ones who grasp the truth.

Jesus' teaching and example are quite different from the attitude reflected in the Old Testament law and some passages in the prophets. But what should we do with these Old Testament verses? A good rule of thumb is to weigh them up against what is known as the golden rule – "do to others as you would have them do to you" (Matthew 7:12) – for this, says Jesus, sums up the law and the prophets. Compassion and love for sinners and outcasts are far more important for Jesus than making sure that we are keeping ourselves pure.

4. Sex-buyers

In the Old Testament, there is no record that men were forbidden from buying sex. However, there are warnings that it might not be wise. In Proverbs 23:27-28, a woman working in prostitution is described as a "deep pit". Men who buy sex are likely to become trapped in something from which they cannot escape – whether it be disease or broken relationships, or a pattern of destructive behaviour they find difficult to stop. Not only that, spending money on prostitution could lead to financial ruin (Proverbs 29:3).

In the New Testament, in 1 Corinthians, Paul gives some startling new teaching. Christian men should not buy sex. Followers of Jesus may not do whatever they want with their bodies, for they are members of Christ (6:15). Sex is not just a physical matter, it has spiritual significance, for when two people join together they become "one flesh". So, transient sexual relationships harm us spiritually, and risk damaging our relationship with Jesus Christ.

In Paul's time in Corinth, a visit to a brothel was considered to be entertainment, just as it is in many places today. Sex could be purchased in brothels and bathhouses, and there was social pressure for men to visit them. So Paul is saying that Christian men should behave differently, and in so doing he challenges the cultural and religious norms. But he goes even further. Whereas in the Old Testament laws, it is the women in prostitution who are considered to be the ones who bring pollution into the community, Paul thinks the men are equally accountable. Expressing a view which was highly counter-cultural and shocking in his time (and still even in ours), he demands that the men of the community take responsibility for their behaviour. There are to be no double standards in the body of Christ.

5. Concluding thoughts

What lessons can we learn from this brief study? First, Christians are always at risk of falling into the trap of complacency, inward looking self-concern and self-righteousness. This has happened to Pastor Joe. He has become more interested in keeping himself and his church pure than in reaching out to and caring for those whom society rejects, and he has found support for this in Scripture. But as we have seen, the Biblical passages which seem to support his views must be weighed up against others which speak of equality and justice. In particular, they must be weighed up against Jesus' teaching of love and compassion. When we look carefully at Scripture as a whole, we see that Pastor Joe's view is mistaken. Justice and mercy are more pleasing to God than congregations which prioritise their own purity and "rightness".

Second, cultural influences are strong, and we may or may not be aware of them. For example, the simplistic view that women are to blame for prostitution has gone unquestioned in many settings for centuries. Such views are reflected in Scripture but they are not allowed the final say. Although the Bible recognises that prostitution is not good for the people involved or society as a whole, it also understands that the issue is much more complex than might at first appear. Cultural tendencies to see women in general as inferior and to shame women in commercial sexual exploitation are questioned, and double standards are challenged, even ridiculed. In the New Testament especially, men are just as responsible for their sexual behaviour as women are – an idea which is still controversial in many parts of the world today!

Lastly, it can be very tempting to take the moral high ground and condemn others, but Scripture does not allow us to do this. If we are to tackle the greed and injustice which cause commercial sexual exploitation we must first recognise and repent of our own idolatries. And if we are to have communities characterised by Christ's love and compassion we have to reach out to all – even, and indeed especially, those who are considered morally and socially unacceptable.

BIBLE STUDY

GENESIS 38

Read the Story of Judah and Tamar

Women in prostitution are often stigmatised and condemned, both by churches and people in general. On the other hand, men are seldom held to account for their behaviour. In the story of Judah and Tamar, the double standards which often apply with regard to prostitution are exposed. Judah's sons have failed to follow the customs of their culture and provide their dead brother's wife with a child. Tamar makes sure that she continues the family line by tricking Judah, her father-in law, into thinking that she is working in prostitution. Tamar is denounced as having played the whore when she is found to be pregnant, and even sentenced to death, but Judah is able to pay for the services of a woman without any recrimination. In the end, however, it is Tamar who is seen to be righteous and used by God, and Judah who is shown up as hypocritical and weak.

QUESTIONS FOR DISCUSSION

> How are women viewed in your cultural setting?
> In the story of Judah and Tamar double standards regarding sexual behaviour and prostitution are exposed. Do you see any double standards in your culture and in your church? If so, how do you think these might be challenged?
> In many cultures, including the Christian church, women in prostitution are often condemned and shunned – why?
> What is the difference between prostitution and commercial sexual exploitation?
> According to Bishop Zac Niringiye poverty is caused by human greed. "The problem is not poverty", he says, "The problem is greed which is a result of idolatry".[24] What do you think of this statement with regard to commercial sexual exploitation?

24. https://www.youtube.com/watch?v=Kzg8uMto6TE

CHAPTER 4

Starting a Ministry

The harvest is plentiful, but the workers are few. Ask the Lord of the harvest to send out workers into the harvest.

Matthew 9:37-8

God does not love us if we change, God loves us so that we can change.

Richard Rohr [25]

1. Introduction

WHEN WE SEE extreme need, it can be very tempting to respond immediately. However, we should try to resist this, and be patient. A great deal of prayer, research and discussion is necessary before we start. This can be a hard lesson to learn, as it was for Emma and Andy. Professionals with demanding jobs, they were inspired by sermons about being adventurous Christians who "expect the unexpected". When they saw the needs on the streets, they decided to leap into action. They made some soup and chocolate brownies, filled huge flasks with tea and coffee, left the kids with Granny, and drove into an area of the city where they knew the women worked. Although they were puzzled when men turned up rather than the women they had been expecting, they felt pleased with themselves. Weren't they doing exactly what Jesus wants – responding to needs and providing food – just like in the story of the feeding of the 5,000? But then Stacey suddenly jumped into their car, and started shouting at them to do something to help her. Her pimp/perpetrator had beaten her up too many times, she said, and he gave her dogfood to eat. Her social worker said she had to make a choice – it was him or her children. Stacey sat in the car, swearing, crying and shouting for an hour. Andy and Emma were scared and hadn't a clue what to do. Should they take her home? Should they take her to their pastor's house? In the end they decided to call the police, and when they arrived it was clear that they

---

[25]. Richard Rohr *Breathing under Water: Spirituality and the Twelve Steps* London SPCK 2016 kindle location 655.

knew Stacey. Andy asked them, "Should we take her to our home?" But suddenly, without warning, Stacey got out to car and started screaming "You f****** Christians are all the same. You give us soup and cakes. Tell us Jesus f******* loves us, but you never actually help! You are all f******useless!" Dismayed, they watched her stumble off and were shocked to see her being kicked and slapped on the face by a man who had been watching her all the time. They were even more shocked, however, when the police started to lecture them on the damage they were causing.

"You are undermining work already done by people who know what they were doing", the policeman said, "and you are putting women like Stacey at even more risk. The last thing we need round here is middle-class do-gooders! And as for taking someone like Stacey home – you could be putting your whole family in danger, not to mention Stacey herself if her pimp comes looking for her!"

*You're all f******* useless!*

Andy and Emma went home, feeling humiliated and bewildered and wondering what had gone wrong. There was no doubt that they had sincere, compassionate hearts. The trouble was they hadn't realised that a knee-jerk response to apparent need is the wrong way to go about things and that a great deal of prayer and discernment is needed if there is to be a sustainable, valuable ministry. With this in mind, in this chapter we will give some hints and pointers which we hope will help avoid the kind of mistake that Andy and Emma made. We will give some guidelines for setting up a ministry which will be lasting and effective.

2. Preparing the ground

Your first priority is prayer. For six months before actually going out onto the streets, take time to meet together and to listen to God. Do this often, to get to know each other and learn how you each relate to God. If you do this, you are much more likely to be united in your work and to get your priorities right. Make prayer the power-house of the ministry. It is imperative that we acknowledge our own weakness, drawing not on our own abilities but on the endless goodness of God. Fasting is also a very powerful spiritual discipline. A struggle can become a victory when self-denial is employed. As Arthur Wallis says in his book *God's Chosen Fast*,

> "When exercised with a pure heart, and a right motive, fasting may provide us with a key to unlock doors where other keys have failed."[26]

Get a map and familiarise yourselves with the area you hope to work in. Go on prayer walks – always going in twos for safety's sake. It is helpful to know something of the history of the area. Has commercial sexual exploitation always been a feature? Is there a history of violence there? This kind of information will help you to gain a feel for the area and the spiritual forces which are at work in it.

Find out as much as you can about the way the women in the area operate. Are they to be found in massage parlours and brothels, or are they working on the streets? Are they from diverse backgrounds – for example, are they local girls or internationals? Are they caught up in addictions to drugs or alcohol? Are they controlled by a pimp or do they work in brothels controlled by a madam? Are they underage? Do they operate alone or in groups? Who are the customers – tourists or businessmen?

Discuss what the aim of the ministry is to be. A crucial issue to be clear about from the beginning is the relationship between evangelism and social activism. In the evangelical tradition, there has been a tendency for these two to become separated. Some have emphasised evangelism, seeing no need for social action, while others have emphasised social action and evangelism has dropped out altogether. But as the Lausanne Covenant of 1974 made clear, "evangelism and socio-political involvement are both part of our Christian duty. For both are necessary expressions of our doctrines of God and Man, our love for our neighbour and our obedience to Jesus Christ."[27] "Integral mission" seeks to bring both evangelism and social responsibility together, and to bring God's love into all areas of life.

Why is this important? If our aim is simply to convert the women, we risk falling into the trap of "scalp hunting" – of seeking conversions for our own satisfaction and sense of achievement. But Christians should never use vulnerable adults to satisfy a desire to make converts – that is religious exploitation. Coercive evangelism is incompatible with the unconditional love which is at the heart of the gospel. Equally, we should not be "rice Christians", who provide food or aid for people only after they have made them hear their message.

There is also a risk of having a "rescue" mentality, in which we believe it is our responsibility to save women from their sin. This has led Christians to make some very serious mistakes in the past. In Ireland in the nineteenth century, for

---

26. Arthur Wallis *God's Chosen Fast: A Spiritual and Practical Guide to Fasting* Fort Washington: CLC Publications 2003, 9.

27. https://www.lausanne.org/content/covenant/lausanne covenant (accessed 29th July 2019)

example, it led to the so-called "Magdalen laundries", in which it was believed that women, through hard work and religious instruction, would be rescued from their "lives of sin" and mend their ways. The reality was, however, that the women were kept in prison-like environments and made to work without pay. In other words, they were being exploited and oppressed. Today, many Christians reach out to the women because of a genuine desire to alleviate their suffering. However, the desire for "rescue" must come from the women themselves, and not be imposed upon them. Moreover, it is not enough simply to help a woman to leave prostitution – we must also have a plan as to how we will support them after they done so. Helping women to leave without a clear strategy can be worse than doing nothing at all.

Vulnerable adults should never be "Christian pimped" as a way of propagating the Christian faith. We are called to love indiscriminately, not to bring evangelistic techniques designed to "save their souls", or make sure that we have done our religious duty. And this means that we have to tackle oppression and injustice, rather than focussing on our own religious comfort. This is something that the prophets often speak about – we can go to church and be involved in worship as much as we like, but neglect of the poor and needy is detestable in God's eyes: "Away with the noise of your songs! I will not listen to the music of your harps. But let justice roll down like a river, righteousness like a never-failing stream!" (Amos 5:23-24).

The Superior Evangelist

There is another reason. People on the margins of society have an uncanny ability to detect unhealthy motivations in those who reach out to them. If they sense that you are targeting them for any reason other than love, they may not respond to you and may even resist you. In the same way, if they sense that you (however unconsciously) think that you are somehow superior to them, your attempts to relate to build genuine relationships with them will be hindered from the outset. If, on the other hand, they see that you regard them as fellow human beings rather than a "project", they are more likely to respond and want to be in relationship with you. As the story of the Magdalen laundries shows, whenever we think that we are morally superior to those we are trying to help, we run the risk of insensitivity, and even cruelty and abuse. Remember that you, too, are broken and weak, and as prone to sin as anyone else. As the Psalmist says, "If you, Lord, kept a record of sins, who could stand?" (Psalm 130:3).

A second important question is: do we have aid or development in mind? Are we trying to help people survive in their current situation, meeting immediate needs (aid) or are we trying to help them leave their desperate situation by offering opportunities for change and enabling them to develop and use their own gifts (development)? While aid is important, there is the possibility, as in Emma and Andy's case, that we become part of the problem rather than the solution. If we simply provide for people's immediate needs without a strategy for long-term transformation we can, as Steve Corbett and Brian Fikkert point out in their book *When Helping Hurts,* disempower the very people we are trying to help, hinder their growth and their ability to effect change in their lives. If, however, we take a "development" approach in which we aim to enable people to change, take responsibility for themselves, and develop and use their gifts, our work will be far more lasting and transformative.

In reality, however, many teams adopt an approach which contains elements of both. For example, although providing a foodbank is technically a form of aid, it can be an effective way of introducing women to the other services we have to offer. This was how we got to know Millie. The only reason her pimp/perpetrator allowed her to come to the drop-in was that he realised he could get free food from our foodbank. Although we didn't like the idea of giving a pimp/perpetrator free food – the upside was that Millie was able to come to the drop-in a couple of nights a week.

Clearly, we need to strike a balance between helping and enabling. But how can we do this? We can learn most from looking at Jesus' approach. He looked after people's physical needs, as the story of the feeding of the five thousand shows (Mt 14: 13-21). But He was also known for being the friend of those whom society rejected. He spent time with them, and ate and drank with them in a way that marked him out as ignoring the social conventions of His day. He identified with those whom religion and society designated as beyond the social pale, and He did this even to the extent that He was called a glutton and a drunkard (Matt 11:19; Lk 7:34). He left it up to those whom he met to decide whether or not they would become his followers. His task was to love them, and to show God's love to them.

3. Starting Out

Once you have come to agreement on your aims in ministry and acquainted yourself with the area you hope to work in, you can start taking more practical steps.

It is important to know what the vision for the project is. It is also important that everyone involved agrees to the vision. Are there plans for a drop-in centre one day? Is it possible to work with local churches and organisations to transform peoples' lives? Devise together a written statement of purpose to which all members of the team subscribe. For example, some aims for a ministry might be:

- To reach out to people involved in commercial sexual exploitation
- To create space (physical, psychological and spiritual) for transformation, exiting and recovery.
- To create and find local solutions for the problems which arise from commercial sexual exploitation.

Formulating aims in this way will help everyone involved to be focused, preventing people working at cross-purposes to each other. If a team becomes fragmented because of a difference in aims, it will not last. A good leader will help the team to understand what the vision is and why it is so important.

Find out if there are projects or agencies already working in the area. Is there a need for the proposed ministry or would you be duplicating something that already exists? Could you join an existing project without having to set up one of your own?

Keep things simple. Achieve one goal before moving on to the next. There is no point in planning to develop a drop-in centre, for example, before you have met and gained the trust of the people you want to use it.

Introduce yourselves to local churches and gain their prayer support for your plans. Listen to the experience and expertise of church leaders, who are likely to have extensive knowledge of the area. Where possible, develop partnerships with them which will be beneficial for all and enable you to work together for the transformation of the area in which you are all operating. As we learn to love and respect each other as followers of Jesus we can create a foretaste of heaven on earth, impacting the community around us. This will also help prepare for long-term relationships and help avoid situations such as the one Lydia found herself in in the last chapter. The church is key in helping people to find healthy relationships with others and with God. Caring, inclusive, servant-hearted and missional churches are crucial for integral mission and in transforming communities. However, some churches, like Pastor Joe's, are still blind to their biblical mandate to bring material and spiritual support to people in need – so you might need patience!

Introduce yourselves to the local police and vice squad and tell them what you hope to do. It is also good to meet community leaders, councillors, local politicians and community workers. They may be sceptical at first, but it is well worth keeping them informed. It is helpful for all team members to have an identity card with his or her photograph on it and the address of your team's base. Identity cards should only give the team member's name and the contact details of your project. Never include personal details such as home address, telephone number or date of birth on identity cards.

Spend some time thinking about the values you want to be foundational to your ministry – for example, treating each person as an individual, with dignity and respect regardless of race, age, gender, sexual orientation social background, criminal history or religious beliefs. Another might be to be enabling rather than controlling, respecting the individual's freedom to make choices.

Our Christian values must be clear and in place before we start doing anything. For example, one group failed to agree at the outset that all team members and volunteers should be believers. A few months down the line, a team member brought along a friend who said she was an atheist but wanted to help out. She was taken on. Trouble started however, when she refused to pray before they set out, and objected when team members told women about Jesus' love for them. A few weeks later arguments arose within the team about the importance of prayer, and some people left.

Know what to expect. Learn as much as you can from people with experience in the field of tackling commercial exploitation.

Think long term. As we learn more about the area, the culture and the people we will be working with, we need to start to think strategically about how we are going to help women. For example, if someone wants to leave commercial sexual exploitation, how are we going to help her? What will her needs be?

Don't be afraid to collaborate with other faith groups and coalitions who have common values and goals with regard to human wellbeing – this can bring fusion and strength into a community. We can work alongside people of different faiths, or none at all, without compromising our commitment to Christ.

4. Forming a Team

At first there may be only two or three of you who wish to start an outreach ministry. However, consistency is important in building up relationships and in order to achieve this you will need to take on others to help you cover holidays and when people are unwell. Wise selection is crucial, for the team's biggest asset is its members. Interview prospective team members using believers whom you know and trust as the interviewers. Make the interview semi-formal, doing as much as you can to make the candidate feel at ease. Request two references, one of which should be from their church pastor or elder. The focus of the interview should be discernment of motivation, experience of working in a team and willingness to learn. Look for people who are willing to be committed for about 5 years – it takes a long time to build up relationships of trust with the women.

Try to make the team as diverse as possible. It is good to have both women and men, from different age groups. It can be very healing for women, who have suffered so much at the hands of pimps and punters, to learn that men can be compassionate, caring and will treat them with respect. It is also helpful to have a man on street outreach teams for safety reasons. Many of the women will come from dysfunctional families, and will find older women easier to speak to, seeing them as safe mothering, and grand-mothering figures.

Similarly, look for people who have different gifts – for example, some who are good with people and can listen well and others who are good at organising. It is essential that all team members are believers. However, it is also helpful to have people from a variety of traditions within the Christian family. No one person or denomination has the monopoly on the truth. An interdenominational team will bring about a continuous sharing of ideas, and we can learn a great deal from each other as we work and pray together. This also helps to avoid falling into a "bunker mentality" in which we begin to think that our way of being Christian is the only one – that "I am right and that everyone else is wrong". As we pray together, the doctrinal and practical differences between us become less significant and we are able to work together for our common purpose.

I know I'm right – God has told me!

5. Learning from our mistakes

Andy and Emma meant well. There was no doubt about their compassion and desire to serve God. The trouble was that they failed to take time to work out how they could best help in the situation. They had no idea what they were getting into, of the kind of people they would be dealing with, or the risks involved. Above all they didn't stop to pray, and it never occurred to them that there might be others out there with experience from which they could learn. Yet God did not allow their work to go to waste. They realised their mistakes and with great humility wrote to the police and apologised, thanking them for their support. Realising that as professional people with a young family they would not be able to sustain a ministry of outreach, they instead developed a prayer group which prayed for the area and supported the team which Lydia was able to start in the area.

BIBLE STUDY

Read Matthew 10: 5-23 (we suggest that you read this in the Message version)

This passage relates Jesus' instructions to his disciples as they are sent out to tell people about him. It contains many invaluable insights into the nature of the task of evangelism, and the fact that we undertake it because we have been given so much. The message of this passage is that our ministry is to be characterised by simplicity, modesty, courtesy, and quietness. Our mission, as Stanley Hauerwas says, "is not to call attention to ourselves, but to Jesus and His kingdom".[28]

QUESTIONS FOR DISCUSSION

> According to this passage, how should we go about reaching out the women? Jesus also warns that our message of love may not always be well received. What forms do you think this reaction is likely to take, and how will you prepare yourselves to handle it?
> Think about how you would like your team to work together – what values are important to you?
> Jesus said, "Blessed are the pure in heart, for they shall see God (Matthew 5:8)". What does being "pure in heart" mean with regard to reaching out to women caught up in commercial sexual exploitation?
> At what point does the desire to help people become harmful to them?
> Why is it important to have diversity within the team?

---

28. Stanley Hauerwas *Matthew* Ada, MI: Brazos Press 2007, 188.

CHAPTER 5

Outreach: Steps in Building Relationships

"I have loved you with an everlasting love; I have drawn you with unfailing kindness."

Jeremiah 31:3

"Just show up!"

Lauran Bethell

1. Introduction

LYDIA WAS DELIGHTED when Tom wanted to work with her. She had known for a while that she needed help, and in particular had been praying that a man would be able to go on outreach with her. The women needed to know that not all men bought sex or were violent. Besides, Lydia had had to admit to herself that she sometimes felt unsafe when she went into the area where the women were working. Sometimes, too, she had felt overwhelmed by the needs of the people she saw as she and her friends prayer-walked the area. It was so good to have someone to discuss things with and make plans. What streets should they concentrate on? When should they go out? Should they take tea, coffee and cakes as Andy and Emma had done?

Questions such as these need to be addressed before going on outreach, and the discussion process is a helpful way to get to know each other. Since good preparation is vital for ministry, in this chapter we will offer some tips and hints to help you do so.

2. Preparing for outreach

Find out when the women are likely to be least busy, with fewer sex buyers around. We need to be prepared to be as flexible in our timing as necessary. It is crucial to be seen to be present, spending time with the women, and getting to know them.

Before going out, pray together. Always tell your support group when you are going out so that they can pray for you. Always work in pairs, never on your own. Carry your identity card at all times. Use a small notebook to keep notes and information. At night, carry a small torch. Take a small Bible in an accessible translation, e.g. the NIV (New International Version) or the Message. Underline appropriate verses and passages. Have a stock of cards which have Scripture verses or prayers on them.

It can be helpful to take hot drinks and cakes with you. When we were out one evening, a chocolate cupcake with pink icing enticed "Esther with the black eye" into staying around and chatting with our team. We learned that she had turned 18 that day, that she had only been working for three weeks but had already been beaten and raped. She never would have imagined she could suffer like this, she said. We were able to tell her that she didn't need to change to be loved by God. We gave her our contact details and a rape alarm, and told her that we would pray for her and could help her to leave if she wanted to. Then her pimp/perpetrator came along, and we had to move on. Our brief encounter was over, but a seed had been sown.

Dress modestly and appropriately for the culture and climate. If it gets cold at night, wear several layers of clothing and watertight boots or shoes. Clothes, make-up and nails can be a talking-point between yourselves and the women you meet – something to talk about and enjoy together.

Arrange to meet other members of the team at regular intervals while you are out. Always know who your team leader is and know where other team members are.

Decide whether or not to give out condoms. This may need prayerful discussion as some Christians believe that contraception is wrong. Some teams work on a "damage limitation" principle– i.e. preventing the spread of disease and unwanted pregnancy. Find out if the women can get condoms from other agencies. Bear in mind, though, that some pimps/perpetrators don't allow women to access health services, and your team may be the only way for them to receive health support.

Clothes and makeup can be a talking point

Have a designated mobile phone for outreach purposes. This number can be given to the women. Decide as a team when you are available to respond to calls or texts. NEVER give out your own private phone number or address, and NEVER invite a woman to your home. Use the phone to contact other team members and emergency services.

At the end of every outreach session, have a debriefing session together (for details, see chapter 6).

If you find that you do not enjoy outreach, or that you dread going out, examine your motives. Should you be serving in some other aspect of the ministry, perhaps behind the scenes in some way?

3. Meeting the women

Explain who you are and why you are there. Tell them that you are Christians. After that, only talk about faith if they are interested. They need to see that you are there out of love for them and not because you want to convert or "rescue" them. Thank them for stopping, for listening. Do all this within a couple of minutes – you are in their working space and they may be in trouble for stopping. That was the case for Stacey (chapter 4) whose pimp/perpetrator had been waiting for her, and slapped and kicked her when she got out of the car. Offer refreshments (e.g. water in summer weather, hot drinks in winter), prayer, rape alarms, Bibles, information on services and team contact details. Remember, however, that gifts can be taken away by the pimp/perpetrator. A good idea is to hand out a good quality lip-gloss with your project's contact details hidden in it.

Ask if they would like to take a drink or a cake for someone else, for example, their pimps or "boyfriends" – this might mean they get permission to talk to you another time. Don't bombard them with questions – we desire relationship, not information. Don't spend too much time with the women or monopolise their attention. Pimps/perpetrators can become violent if the think the women are shirking or failing to earn money.

First impressions are important – and lasting. Women who are caught in commercial sexual exploitation are very astute, and they develop quick assessment skills in order to survive.

If you are planning to go into clubs or brothels, gain the permission of the owner or manager before you do so. Take gifts and information about your organisation. If the owner lets you in, sit for a while having drinks, making yourselves available to chat, and hand out the gifts. If you are not allowed in, ask the manager if you can leave the gifts for the women.

We need to have patience and be consistent – becoming a familiar presence in the area. Trust and respect cannot be assumed or demanded, but must be built up over time. Going out once a week on the same day is far more effective than going out twice in one week and not at all the next. Sometimes you may meet many women, sometimes none at all. Sometimes women will want to spend time with you and talk, sometimes not. As Lauran Bethell says, three-quarters of the battle in establishing a ministry is to keep showing up!

Inevitably, there will be crisis situations which need immediate attention, but in general, try to keep a mindset of befriending, rather than one which is task-led. It is easy to fall into the trap of being task-oriented, but this will ultimately undermine relationship building. In many settings there are plenty of agencies whose main task is to meet physical, social and even financial needs. You are different! You are bringing the light of Jesus into a dark, abhorrent area – something that no statutory body or secular agency can do.

We should not make claims about what we (or others) can do for the women. This might make us feel better in the moment, but failure to deliver will only be another devasting blow from a 'do-gooder' who has done no good whatsoever. So many of the women have had things promised to them, and have been let down – so say what you mean and mean what you say.

If a woman shares personal concerns with you – for example, about her background or housing problems – offer to pray for her and seek her permission to share this with others who pray. Assure her of confidentiality.

Remember that every woman we meet, no matter how broken she may appear, is made in the image of God. We are called to touch people's lives as He does, with unconditional love.

Give women space to talk and be an attentive listener. Practise active listening:

- **Reflect** back rather than evaluate
- **Clarify** rather than confront
- **Support** rather than attempt to problem-solve
- **Develop** rather than analyse
- **Share silence** rather than fill in the gaps in conversation
- **Summarise** rather than interpret

Be patient! It may take some time before you meet any women, let alone build up relationships with them. Perseverance is key.

Be imaginative in your outreach. For example, give gifts at Christmas, eggs at Easter, flowers on Mother's Day and International Women's Day.

4. Follow-Up

We may feel it is appropriate to meet some women outside outreach time. As we gain experience, we become able to discern who is interested in continuing with contact and those for whom we seem to be simply another "social service". Avoid making appointments in response to crises – this could convey the message that a woman is only worthy of attention if there are problems to be solved. Always consult with a colleague and pray with them before you commit to an individual woman.

Arrange to meet the woman in a café. Meeting on "neutral territory" will increase the woman's sense of security and encourage her to speak freely with you. Be sure to keep the appointment, but don't be surprised if she does not. You might have many "no shows" at first, but it is important that they learn that you are reliable and consistent in relationship. If a woman misses an appointment, don't probe as to why – just accept that she was unable to make it and proceed from there.

Meeting up for coffee

A key question to ask as you offer support is: "How can I help?" Avoid telling here what she needs to do: we can unconsciously bring our agenda into the situation without listening to what is really concerning the women.

Keep in touch through texts and cards. However, don't give any confidential information in texts because you cannot be sure who may have access to the phone and you could put her or others at risk.

Before the meeting, arrange roles with your outreach partner. One might deal with social and physical problems, and the other with spiritual mentoring. Establishing roles will help the woman understand the boundaries of relationships.

Allow approximately 90 minutes for the first meeting. As you begin to build up the relationship, don't focus on the rights or wrongs of commercial sexual exploitation. It's better to start with the obvious "painkillers" she is using e.g. drugs, alcohol or unhealthy, damaging relationships, as she is likely to be preoccupied with the things she wants to change and how to get help, rather than with how she can stop working.

Assess the practical issues. For example, she may need housing or rehab, or be worried about debt. Other topics might include:
- Family – isolation, rejection, children, abandonment
- Drugs and rehabilitation possibilities

- Benefits claims and welfare rights
- Outstanding court cases
- Housing
- Health issues, including drug related problems
- Debt
- Spirituality
- Danger of violence

It is useful to have a small card with emergency numbers such as social work services, hospitals, rehabilitation units, housing officers etc. If you are aiming to help with any problem such as housing or health, try to help her set realistic goals with reasonable timescales.

Arrange to meet up regularly. Even if you only meet once a fortnight or once a month, this will promote constructive routines. When appropriate, encourage women to contact other agencies, be they statutory or non-statutory.

If appropriate, work together with the woman to devise a care plan and set goals. If the woman expresses a desire to leave commercial sexual exploitation, discuss with her how this can be done safely. Ask God to give you wisdom as to what the priorities should be. As we work with the woman, we should always refer to the care plan.

Always ask permission before praying with a woman. If she agrees, pause for a little and ask God to reveal to you what you should pray for or about. Keep your prayers general rather than specific. Don't pray AT, pray FOR. The women will listen intently to your prayers, so don't make predictions in them, or use them as opportunities to tell the women indirectly what you think they should be doing. Where possible encourage them to pray for themselves. It is helpful to say something like "what would you like to say to God?"

After the meeting, write a report and store in a confidential location and pass on all action points to the relevant team leader.

5. Relationship Building

As we meet with individual women regularly, we get to know them – their likes and dislikes, and their habits. Some will let us down, others may disappear. We may have to forgive "seventy-seven times" (Mt 18:21-22) or recognise that someone we are working with no longer wants to meet us, and have to let go. With experience, we learn how to gauge people and situations, and to recognise half-truths and exaggerations.

Many who are involved in commercial sexual exploitation adopt different personas to help them survive. For example, a woman may tell us a different name every time we meet her and refuse to tell us her real name. This is a self-protection mechanism adopted by people whose bodies and freedom are constantly being invaded. However, it is possible for a woman to adopt so many personae that she forgets who she really is. When a woman does this, it can signify the beginning of a disintegration in her sense of identity. Don't insist that the woman tell you her real name – she will do so when she is ready, when she feels she can trust you not to abuse the power that knowing a person's name gives another.

Adhere to the team's confidentiality policy. If you think it necessary to break a confidence, ask yourself the following questions:

- Will the woman perceive it as beneficial if a professional body has access to this information?
- Is it necessary to do so for legal reasons, for example, with the police or social workers?
- Is breaking the confidence bringing light into the situation?

Who am I?

- Am I keeping silent because I am afraid that the woman will reject me?
- Am I disclosing information in order to look good in other peoples' eyes?
- Am I just enjoying a gossip?

Be aware of transference and counter-transference. Transference takes place when the person you are working with transfers onto you (the helper) feelings which she had for an important person in her childhood. This can be positive or negative. For example, she might resent or fear you because you remind her of someone who was cruel to her in the past, or become fond of you because she sees you as a mother-figure. Either way, the important thing is to be aware of this, and neither to exploit it nor allow it to develop into something that is unhealthy. Similarly, you should be aware of your own reactions and feelings for the woman you are working closely with (counter transference), and be willing to explore them when you are discussing things with your supervisor and prayer partners. Always be on the alert for over-dependency – on the part of the woman, but especially yourself.

Keep healthy boundaries. Saying "no" does not necessarily mean a lack of love on your part. You cannot always be the one who is there to listen or do things for her. If there is anything that she can do for herself, then she should do it.

Avoid **co-dependency**. It is possible to become too dependent on a relationship. Co-dependency happens when your motivation for becoming involved in people's lives becomes distorted. Melodie Beattie defines a co-dependent person as follows:

> "A person who has let someone else's behaviour affect him or her and is obsessed with controlling other people's behaviour"[29]

Co-dependency is a common reaction in people who live or work with people who have addictions. They become completely absorbed in trying to stop the addict behaving in destructive ways. That is, they take on responsibility for the person's behaviour. Another aspect of this is becoming emotionally dependent on the person for whom they are caring. This tends to happen to people who have a "need to be needed". They need to have someone to help in order to feel good about themselves. The relationship becomes more important for the helper's wellbeing than it is for the person who is being helped. In these cases, when the relationship ends, it is far more upsetting for the helper than the other. The key question about co-dependency is whose needs are being served when you are helping someone?

Some further warning signs of possible co-dependency are:
- Being unable to have a realistic view of the other's faults
- Becoming defensive about the relationship
- Not wanting to share ministry in the relationship with anyone else
- Becoming preoccupied with the person
- Spending so much time with the person that other relationships suffer
- Speaking for the other person without consulting them
- Making decisions for them
- Wanting to be liked
- Becoming too upset when the relationship cools off

One of the biggest hazards of working with any group of people, is the risk of being manipulated. Manipulation refers to behaviour which is designed to control you, to make sure that the person gets what she wants out of the relationship. Some people do this quite openly, by threatening and bullying. But manipulation can be very subtle, and you may not even be aware that it is happening. Here are some examples of behaviour which may be described as manipulative:
- Giving gifts for no good reason
- Eye contact – meaningful looks at another when they are displeased
- Flattery – "I don't know what I would do without you!"; "You are the best worker on the team".

---

29. Melodie Beattie *Co-Dependent no More: How to Stop Controlling Others and Start Caring for Yourself* (2nd edition) Center City: Hazelden 1992.

- Private jokes – exclusive talk
- Exaggerating needs in order to gain sympathy
- Making the other person feel guilty "You wouldn't do that if you really cared about me"
- Cold silences
- Playing one member of the team off against the other

Recognising manipulation is a matter of experience. Some people have an instinct which tells them when they are being manipulated, others are less intuitive and less able to spot the signs. If you find yourself responding to a request with "It goes against my better judgement, but..." – stop and think.

All personal relationships are risky. You may well be hurt. However, our reliance is on God who never changes and whose love for us is beyond our comprehension. Ultimately, our dependency should be on him.

> The Lord is my strength and my defence;
> He has become my salvation.
> He is my God, and I will praise him,
> My father's God, and I will exalt Him (Exodus 15:2)

6. Developing a drop-in centre

After you have been established for some time and have got to know the women in the area, you may want to provide a drop-in centre – a safe place in which the women can come and relax, meet team members, and begin to discover new possibilities. Once you have found a suitable place, try to make the atmosphere as comfortable as possible. If you can, decorate the premises in a non-institutionalised, culturally appropriate, warm and welcoming way.

Some of the things you might offer in the drop-in are
- showers
- washing machines
- hot drinks
- clothing and toiletries
- information about services and agencies.
- counselling and prayer rooms.
- rape alarms and condoms
- activities such as art, sewing, beauty and music
- literacy training and language learning
- food bank

From the outset, have clear rules as to when and how long to be open, and stick to a routine. Opening hours will depend on the needs of the women. The more chaotic their lives are the more likely it is that you will have to be open late at night.

This should be a place where unconditional love is expressed, but where boundaries as to what is acceptable and unacceptable behaviour are clear. There should be no drug-taking or dealing on the premises and no pimps/perpetrators, madams or clients should be allowed in. Sometimes trouble will arise. For example, one evening Millie (chapter 4) picked a fight with another woman and started shouting and swearing. She refused to stop shouting and eventually had to be asked to leave. The episode upset everyone and spoiled the whole evening. If something like this happens, let the team leader take charge, and do what she says. Unless you are in leadership, don't discuss altercations that take place on the streets or in the drop-in with the women.

The key is "welcome, welcome, welcome". Keep communication as personal as possible, and authentic. For example, if you haven't seen a woman for a long time and you are delighted when she comes to the door, say something like, "I am so pleased to see you tonight. It's been too long! Thank you so much for coming!" But if someone like Millie comes to the door, and you don't genuinely feel pleased to see her, it is appropriate to say something like "You are welcome here. Thank you so much for coming. Come in and have a hot drink." The crucial difference is that the word "I" is missing from your communication with Millie. We are being welcoming and authentic with both women, but being less personal with Millie, until there can be a restoration of relationships.

Be respectful of individuality. Try to remember details like favourite drinks – tea with three sugars? Hot chocolate? Try to remember previous conversations and follow up on them without being intrusive. The message must be "You are loved, valued, and worth knowing." In conversation, remember that you are not there to gain information but to build up trust and to enable them to experience the presence of God.

Encourage the women to make decisions. Choosing what food to take from a food bank might seem trivial to us, but for people whose lives are controlled by others, the need to choose can be crippling. If they learn to trust their judgement about these small things, they may one day be able to trust enough to decide to leave commercial sexual exploitation altogether.

BIBLE STUDY

Read Luke 15:1-7
The Parable of the Lost Sheep

This story speaks of God's great love for all his people, and of his anguish when one becomes lost. The religious leaders have been grumbling that Jesus spends time having dinner with sinners, apparently thinking that he should be keeping more respectable company. Jesus responds by telling the story of the shepherd who sets out to find one sheep who has got lost. He makes the point that everyone is valuable to God, without exception. Furthermore, God pursues the lost sheep and carries it to safety on his shoulders.

> The parable of the lost sheep speaks of God's love for those who stray away from safety, and the need for the shepherd to go looking for them. How can you go about showing the women that they are precious in God's sight?

> Shepherds need to take care of themselves as they do their work. What strategies have you put in place to protect yourselves as you reach out to those who are lost?

> Have you ever experienced co-dependency, either in yourself or in others? How was the situation resolved?

> When, if ever, should confidentiality be broken?

> Why is it important never to give out personal details or invite the women to your home?

CHAPTER 6

Leadership and Teamwork

And He said to me, "My grace is sufficient for you, for my power is made perfect in weakness".

2 Corinthians 12:9

1. Introduction

AT THE BEGINNING of a project, there is a sense of being part of something which is exciting and important. It's "all hands on deck" as people work together to see the vision come to fruition. As things settle down, and routine sets in, problems can appear, as Lydia and Tom found out. They had been going out on outreach regularly once a week for a while, had built up a small team, and were now recognised and increasingly accepted by the women. They even had a small room in a church which they were able to use as a drop-in. However, just as the ministry seemed to be making progress, trouble started. One team member had to pull out because of ill-health, and another became unreliable – she kept promising she would be there but then wouldn't show up. Team meetings became difficult, as personalities began to clash. New people had to be taken on. Knowing that their biggest asset was the people who were working with them in ministry, Lydia and Tom realised they had to learn new skills of leadership which would enable them to get through these teething troubles and grow the kind of team that was required to work towards their vision. What kind of information would help them to do this? Teamwork is never easy, but when everyone puts in the effort, it is extremely rewarding. In this chapter we will take you through some information and guidance on building healthy and effective teams.

2. More on Team Work: Relationships

In the 1960's psychologist Bruce Tuckman described a pattern which he saw in teams as they developed. The five stages are forming – storming – norming

– performing- adjourning.[30] A good team leader can be more effective if she knows that this pattern can occur and knows how to steer the group through them. But each team member also has a responsibility to behave in a way that is conducive to working together.

Forming. At the beginning of the team's life, and as they get to know each other, people are enthusiastic and polite. Roles and responsibilities are often unclear at this stage. Team members are content to follow the directive of the leader. The leader's task at this stage is to help the team identify goals in line with the original vision.

Forming a team

Storming. In this stage people are beginning to settle into their roles and become competent in them. They may want to develop the role further and so begin to push against the early boundaries which have been established. Leaders can be challenged, cliques formed, and team members push against each other and become disaffected. Different styles of working become obvious. Personality clashes and theological differences can become evident. There is a need for the clarification of roles. Team leaders help to calm relationships and conflicts and help to build up trust.

Norming. In this stage team members are finally established in their roles and want to get on with the work. If the team has managed to get through the storming phase, the leader is respected and differences are resolved. Others' strengths are appreciated and collaboration can take place. Procedures can be clarified and set down and plans made.

Performing. At this stage a rhythm of working together has been established and each member works within their strengths. When disagreements occur, they can be constructively resolved and there is healthy peer support. Procedures work well, and changes in personnel do not disrupt performance.

30. Bruce Tuckman "Developmental Sequence in Small Groups" <u>Psychological Bulletin</u> 63 (1965)

There is a fifth stage (**adjourning**) which comes about when the specific task is completed and the group is no longer necessary. There is a sense of achievement but, for some, also stress and insecurity about the future and a sense of loss.[31]

In the "all hands on deck" phase, individual gifts tend to be less evident and important and but as things settle down, talents need to be identified and developed so that individuals and teams can flourish. It may take some time to identify the best fit for someone. Not everyone will be suitable for going out on to the streets, and someone who is gifted in fundraising, for example, may not be good at listening or intercession. Once your team members' gifts have been identified, establish boundaries. Everyone in the team should be sure of his or her job description and role, and know who the team leader is. This will help avoid confusion and conflict.

In small teams, weaknesses can be more evident, as people may have to take on tasks for which they are not well suited. As your team grows it will be easier for people to work according to their strengths, and it is a leadership responsibility to enable them to do so. As a team ask yourselves: what has God said to us? What are our priorities? How much can we do as individuals? What are the time constraints? Learn to respect diversity of gifts, and different ways of working. People can become weary when they are being asked to work in areas for which they do not have a gift.

In Romans 12:14-16, Paul gives wise advice about the kind of attitudes we should have towards one another if we are to work effectively together: "Bless your enemies; no cursing under your breath. Laugh with your happy friends when they're happy; share tears when they're down. Get along with each other; don't be stuck-up. Make friends with nobodies; don't be the great somebody" (The Message).

Divisions within teams is a major threat to mission. Jesus prayed that his disciples would be unified for the sake of mission (John 14). For the sake of the Kingdom, we need to put aside differences of doctrine and practice and the need to feel that our way is the only right way.

Make a commitment to resolve team conflict as and when it happens. Remember Jesus' teaching that if our brother or sister has something against us, we should make seeking reconciliation a priority (Matthew 5:23-24).

Be careful of your speech: gossip will kill the team. It will cause division and offence, and trust will be lost (Proverbs 16:28; Romans 1:29; 2 Cor 12:20).

Be spiritually accountable. If one person feels strongly that they have heard from God on an aspect of the project's work, this should be brought to the team leader and the wider group for discernment. If this is not done, spiritual arrogance can set in which destroys team life and only leads to strife. 1 John 4:1 speaks of "discerning the spirits", and warns against failing to test what we think we are

---

31. Bruce Tuckman & Mary Ann C. Jensen "Stages of Small Group Development Revisited" Group Facilitation 10 (2010), 43-48.

receiving from God: "Dear friends, do not believe every spirit, but test the spirits to see whether they are from God, for many false prophets have gone out into the world" (1 John 4:1).

Service users will detect tensions amongst team members. They will sense immediately if there is distrust amongst those who are working with them. They will also sense immediately if there is dishonesty or manipulation. It can be very helpful from time to time to have outside observers and facilitators helping the team to recognise its own dynamics, strengths and weaknesses and blind spots.

It can be a useful exercise to encourage team members to draw up their own job description, modifying them as the team matures and individuals' strengths and interest become evident.

Each team member should have a support group of at least two people who meet to pray for his or her personal and spiritual needs. These should be spiritually mature people whom the team member respects, who will listen well and speak the truth, and be supportive in times of discouragement.

Be sensitive to differing perspectives within your team and allow these to have a voice. For example, men are often very much in the minority, and those who do volunteer can have a quite different experience from female team members. Here's what Jason said a few months after getting involved:

They will sense disunity

"In all honesty, it's the most uncomfortable thing I've ever done. I'm out of my depth and have never had an experience like it. But despite all my discomforts, the knowledge that God has called me to this, that this is where God's heart is, and the privilege of being a part of something that few men have, makes it all worthwhile! I feel a deep sense of frustration and responsibility as a man! We were meant to be protectors of women – not to abuse them and certainly not to look away from the abuse. God is more than able to turn this around, but we men need to stand up against it, not leave it to other women to do it alone!"

A willingness to listen to each other and to understand differing points of view and experience will produce a much stronger team which can minister in humility and mutual support.

3. Tips for team leadership

Planned meetings, good time-keeping and giving everyone a voice are crucial for a healthy and productive team. Each team meeting should have an agenda and everyone should know what the aim of the meeting is. Devise good communication strategies: outreach rotas and regular meetings help ensure that everyone knows what is going on.

Lack of good team dynamics and clear objectives contribute to chronic stress. Organisational plans are more achievable when there are strong relationships and consultative leadership. Ministries flourish when there is low control and creativity is encouraged.

Working with others can be hard. It requires respect, patience and sometimes hard decisions must be made. Inappropriate or unhealthy behaviour from team members needs sensitive and wise handling. Lydia and Tom found it very tricky to deal with one of their team who refused to adhere to policies everyone had agreed to. She was a great listener and the women trusted her. However, she disagreed with the rule about not inviting the women to her home, and persisted in doing so even though she was specifically requested not to. After painful discussions and much heart-searching, it was felt they had to let her go.

Everyone in the team should have a clearly defined role. Allocating team members as key workers can go a long way to keeping the work organised and manageable. But sometimes needs are overwhelming and immediate, and we cannot all be available all of the time. When I (Ruth) was working at the Earl's Court Project in London (a joint venture between Holy Trinity Brompton Church and YWAM) in the 1980's, many women were ill with the HIV/AIDS virus. We wanted to be the hands and feet of Jesus in what seemed like a tsunami of pain, but our small team was not coping. There were so many emergencies, how could we prioritize? We discussed how we could respond and came up with an idea. I imagined a stone (representing Jesus and his flow of love) being thrown into a pond and three ripples coming out from it. On the innermost circle we named the women whose needs we considered would be

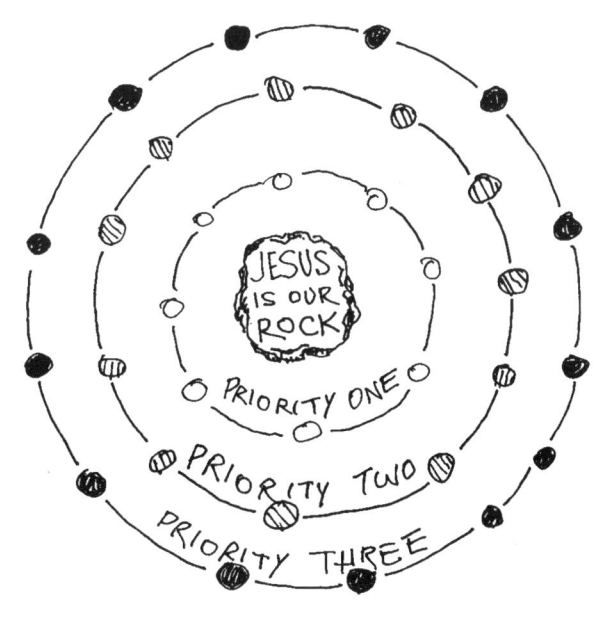

Rock diagram

most urgent, with the others less being assigned to levels two and three. There were five of us front line workers and we all had varying degrees of relationship with different women. Each team member put his or her number (1,2,3,4,5,) against the name of a woman with whom he or she felt had a relationship. Not everyone knew or felt a call to every woman, but by God's grace, every name had more than one number beside it. So, if Sarah, for example, needed help but her usual worker wasn't around, there would be another who had committed to take over in the absence of that particular team member. This meant that when an emergency arose, we did not waste time wondering who should respond – it was already decided. This helped alleviate the strong feelings of guilt that often arose because everyone felt that they should be responding to every need, every time.

Remember that vulnerability can be your strongest point. It is when we are weak that God works through us (2 Cor 12:9).

Don't be afraid of getting things wrong. God wants us to learn from our mistakes and trials. If we can work through the problems, we will grow and mature and have a deeper self-awareness and humility. This will lead us into greater accountability, wisdom and fruitfulness as God can work through us. Often, we try to seek relief from our vulnerabilities and weaknesses by making others pay the price for them. If we feel weak, we blame someone else; if we feel powerless, we bully, if we feel small, we can take out our rage on another. The good news is that God uses our mistakes and even our sin as an opportunity for us to grow and for him to pour out his grace: "Did they stumble so far as to fall beyond recovery? Not at all! Rather, because of their transgression, salvation has come..." (Romans 11:11)

Listen to criticism – even, and perhaps especially, from the team.

Decide on your priorities and act on them. This will mean that you have to make choices – you can't do everything. As J. Oswald Sanders says: "The leader must be meticulously careful in selection of priorities...If there is ambition to excel there must be selection and rejection in order to concentrate on what is of paramount importance."[32]

Ambition for the work of the team is important, but be wary of personal ambition – it kills teamwork and it will kill our ministry. It is good to have goals and to want to be obedient in the calling God has given us. However, the desire for power over others will take us away from God's purposes (see Mark 10:35-45). As soon as one person seeks to supersede another, jealousy and resentment set in. Of course, it is necessary that some people will assume roles and positions which involve authority over others, but those in this situation must view themselves in terms of servant leadership, rather than "over and against others". Each person in the team is under

---

32. J. Oswald Sanders *Spiritual Leadership: Principles of Excellence for Every Believer* Chicago: Moody Publishers 2007, page 87.

the Lordship of Christ and whatever role we play in the team we are all equal before him. Leadership is about role, not about status. It is also important to respect each other's roles and not to encroach on each other's area of responsibility.

Avoid perfectionism. Many Christians think that when Jesus says "Be perfect, therefore, as your heavenly Father is perfect" (Matthew 5:48) he means that we have to strive for perfection in all that we do. But the Greek word here is *teleioi*, which means "mature", or "complete". Jesus therefore is asking here that we grow up, become mature, complete in him – not that we have a perfect ministry. In order to do this we need to start with love for God, with healthy self-awareness and a continuous willingness to learn. We need to give up any dreams we may have of pioneering the perfect ministry – it won't happen.

Compulsive perfectionism, either in ourselves as individuals or collectively as a team, comes from a deep sense of insecurity, fear of failure and is borne out of a need to have the approval of others.[33]

Be accountable – to your support group, your team and where appropriate, your own seniors in the organisation. When leaders fail, it is often when they are operating in isolation.

If you find yourself in a culture different to your own or working in a multicultural team, take special care to "bear one another's burdens" (Galatians 6:2) and be gracious about difference. Don't be quick to take offence (Ecclesiastes 7:9) but try to understand why others behave or speak as they do. Where possible, try to build up a "bank" of trusted people who would be able to translate for women who do not speak the language of the area in which you are working.

4. Managing change

Sooner or later, teams have to cope with change – in ourselves, in others and in our work. Physician Paul Tournier says, "We must always be letting go what we have acquired, and acquiring what we do not possess, leaving one place in order to find another, abandoning one support in order to reach another, turning our backs on the past to thrust wholeheartedly towards the future."[34]

It is comfortable to be in the norming and performing stage – we know what we are doing and feel secure. But when team members leave, for whatever reason, or if the project expands, objectives are modified and new people taken on, difficulties can arise. Dealing with change, even when the need for expansion is due to the team's success, can be very difficult. For example, Angela couldn't join in with the excitement and encouragement felt by others when outreach was increased from two nights to four, and the team expanded. She knew that growth was needed and could

---

33. Will Van Der Hart & Rob Waller *The Perfectionism Book: Walking the Path to Freedom* London: IVP 2016

34. Paul Tournier *A Place for You: Psychology and Religion* Harper & Row 1968, 164.

only be good for the women, but the changes made her feel confused and lonely. She started to criticise the project to other team members in an attempt to feel some kind of connection. After six months Angela left – no longer the positive, enthusiastic, faithful, empathetic front-line worker she had once been. She refused the offer of a de-brief meeting with a non-team member, though she accepted an affirming prayer-time accompanied with cards, presents and flowers from her colleagues.

Making plans

Change is associated with a wealth of reactions and emotions: people can feel frustrated, confused, purposeless, useless, and even bereaved. This may not be acknowledged or recognised. Teams can be so vocal on their successes that team members who have a sense of loss can feel alone and unable to express their feelings. It is part of the team leader's role to help people work through this change, recognise the stresses and express their feelings. In the short term, this can be very painful, but it will pass.

So look out for the way people are coping with change. Marion Knell lists four unhealthy ways of coping with change:

- Denying that there is a problem or ignoring unpleasant feelings.
- Suppression. Pushing feelings down into the subconscious where they remain buried until triggered by a later event.
- Withdrawal. Finding forms of escapism that enable you to avoid the reality of the situation. Staying indoors, refusing to interact with the environment, or finding excuses for not meeting people.
- Rationalization. Finding plausible reasons for feeling the way you do without treating the root causes.[35]

Knell is writing about the stress of returning home after a period of service overseas, but this list can equally apply to other kinds of change. The important thing is for team leaders to know that people react to change differently and some struggle

35. Marion Knell *Burn Up or Splash Down, Surviving the culture Shock of Re-Entry* Atlanta: Authentic 2007, 31.

more than others. Encourage people to talk about it, if not with the team leader or other team members, with their prayer partners or support group.

5. Debriefing

It is increasingly recognised that psychosocial support is important for frontline workers who reach out to complex and deeply traumatised victims and perpetrators involved in commercial sexual exploitation. A major way to care for people is to hold a regular, short debrief after every outreach or drop-in session before everyone goes home. We will have more to say about this in chapter 7 ("Resilience in Ministry") but in the meantime, here are some hints. At the end of the session, gather everyone together to talk about what has happened and to pray. Encourage one another with positive stories. Ask yourselves these questions:

1. Where did I encounter the presence of God? What was good?
2. What was challenging? Did I sense evil?
3. Did I hear any information about children? Are there any child protection issues that will have to be reported? (this is particularly important when you are working in countries where there is a statutory obligation to report abuse or neglect of children).

This need not take long, as people will be anxious to get home, particularly if it is late. Nevertheless, making debrief part of your routine after outreach, drop-in sessions and critical incidents sends a strong message to your team members that they are valued and cared for. Volunteers and team members deserve the most supportive work settings and systems we can provide. The debrief should be led by someone who is familiar with and understands the team's objectives. Sometimes, though, there may not be enough time at the end of an outreach session or drop-in to share and articulate the impact of what has happened, especially if the session has been particularly difficult. If so, arrange to see the team member later in the week, and talk through the incident with her. De-briefing is an opportunity for her to tell the story from her perspective and articulate feelings. Some people find writing about the incident and their feelings beneficial, rather than talking about them.

If an emergency or traumatic event occurs, spend some time afterwards in de-briefing and discussing any changes which will improve future practice. Sometimes an outreach worker can be competent during a crisis but still benefit from de-brief three or even four days later, rather than straight away. People under extreme stress are not able to assess their own needs. Professional help at an early stage can help to resolve issues more satisfactorily and prevent long-term distress. It can help prevent depression or anxiety disorders from developing and it can deal with feelings of failure or guilt.[36]

36. For more on this, see chapter 8.

BIBLE STUDY

Read Romans 12:3-8 (Message translation)
Using our Gifts

Working together as a team is difficult and requires co-operation, sacrifice and patience on everybody's part. In Romans 12 Paul warns against thinking too highly of our own abilities or lording it over others. He also reminds us that Christians are part of the body of Christ, and that we have different gifts and tasks – both spiritual and practical. In any group, Christians should be encouraged and enabled to exercise the gifts that God has given them, and to do this to the best of their ability.

QUESTIONS FOR DISCUSSION

> Why does Paul think humility is so important?
> What gifts do your team members have? Do you think that they are being put to good use?
> What experience of teamwork do you have? What worked well and what didn't work so well?
> What qualities should a good leader have?
> How would you go about helping people to cope with change in the team and its work?

CHAPTER 7

Management and Governance

"My presence will go with you and I will give you rest."
Then Moses said to Him, "If your presence does not go with us, do not send us up from here"

Exodus 33: 14-15.

1. Introduction

LYDIA AND TOM'S team was flourishing, and their work was becoming known and respected. Women were referred to them by other agencies, and others were coming for help of their own volition. A couple of local churches were very supportive, supplying soup and cakes for outreach, and providing a hall for a drop-in once a week. More people wanted to be part of the team, which meant that they were able to meet more women outside of outreach times. Lydia and Tom were delighted that things were going so well, but they also began to find themselves over-stretched. Gradually, the work grew so much that they found they had to think about taking on staff: full-time project workers, people to do administrative tasks and someone to raise funds. They needed office space and equipment, and to have safe premises from which to work. The drop-in in the church hall was great, but they realised they needed to find their own premises so that they could open up more often. Whereas before they had been team leaders, now they found themselves in positions of management with responsibilities they had not expected to have. There was so much more to learn.

This chapter suggests some guidelines and practices which we hope will help you to develop your ministry if it gets to a stage when things need to be more formalised. Please note that they are only guidelines. We write from experience, but we are aware that not everything will be workable or applicable in your setting. From now on we will make a distinction between "staff" and "volunteers" within a team as a whole.

2. Becoming an employer

Ask God to reveal His operational plans and procedures, then stick to them.

Make sure that you adhere to employment law, both locally and where the charity is registered. Ensure that staff have a reasonable wage, a contract of employment, job description, health insurance, holiday entitlement and pension provision. Employees will need equipment – e.g. a desk, telephone, computer. Agree on working hours (start times, lunch breaks etc) at the outset in accordance with the nature of the role.

Much of what we have already said about team-work applies here too. Everyone on the team needs to have clear vision and purpose with well specified roles which are known to all. Be committed to and value diversity in your team – in gender, age, social background, ethnicity and Christian tradition.

Work premises will have to be clean, safe, with fire safety measures in place, and equipment in good working order. Make sure your employees know that their welfare is important to you and to the organisation as a whole. Health and safety law will vary from country to country – so make sure you know what the legislation is.

Never underestimate the importance of a properly conducted selection process to ensure the right person is selected as a member of staff or volunteer. Often projects take short cuts when there are acute shortages of personnel. It doesn't work! People taken on in haste very often leave soon after. Ask team members to feedback knowledge from their experience which will help create good job specifications.

Equipment should be in good working order

If there is a high attrition rate (i.e. if too many people seem to be leaving), then it is important to find out why. People will always leave for personal reasons, but if they are leaving because they are unhappy with the work, something needs to be done. Have open and honest discussion to clarify what the difficulties are. It may help to have an objective outsider help you to identify the problem.

According to research carried out amongst missionary bodies, larger organisations tend to retain staff and volunteers longer than smaller ones.[37] Perhaps this is because the need for policies and procedures in place is greater in larger organisations and leaders are more attuned to the need for caring for people. But leaders of small teams can do a great deal to keep people on board. Good, consistent communication, and a simple "thank you" go a long way.

Taking time for prayer and regular retreats is crucial. Retreats should focus on spirituality rather than work. One project we know of, which was receiving government funding, was facing severe pressure to provide frontline services. The pressure was such that Emily, the leader, was worried that the team might crack under the strain. Wages were low, resources inadequate, the work was dangerous and staff and volunteers were all overstretched. Yet the team members had all been in post for over five years. Why were they staying? A review by an outside organisation revealed that the quarterly retreat for office and frontline staff always refreshed them. Often, they went to these retreats under protest because there was so much work to do. Yet God always met them with kindness, and individuals and relationships were healed in deeper levels as they walked in His presence. Emily encouraged honesty, seeing it as positive, even when it seemed negative!

Ensure that frontline workers have regular supervision (see chapter 7). Conduct annual appraisals for all staff. It is imperative that staff have space to shape and develop their own ministry.

Develop a detailed manual with clear guidelines, protocols and policies (see below) and make it available for everyone to read. Procedures protect us against being "reactors" rather than people who build up and equip team members over time. Often when there are relationship breakdowns and challenges because of incompetence, there is also a history of bending procedures and policies to place an individual in post too soon.

Establish prayer support for the work of the team and keep supporters informed of developments. It helps to produce a newsletter regularly and post non-confidential news and prayer points on social media.

3. More notes on leadership

Delegate. In Numbers 11:44, Moses realised that he could not do everything himself and delegated many duties to teams. We should follow Moses' example! We cannot, and should not, attempt to do everything ourselves.

Don't be afraid to be vulnerable – people will see through you anyway. Be accessible to your staff, teachable and gracious. Set a good example with regard

---

37. Rob Hay, Valerie Lim, Detlef Blöcher, Jaap Katelaar & Sarah Hay *Worth Keeping: Global Perspectives on Best Practice in Missionary Retention* Pasadena, CA: William Carey Library 2007, 39.

to work-life balance. As the project grows, keep an eye on your motives. Personal ambition can take us away from God's will and our true calling. The purpose of our work is to exalt God, not ourselves. In God's kingdom "the last will be first, and the first will be last" (Matthew 20:16). Leadership in the kingdom is servant leadership and we are not to lord it over others. Remember that in God's upside-down kingdom, character is more important than action or tasks.

Leadership is often a matter of juggling the needs of people, the human and spiritual task entrusted to us and the organisational requirements which arise from and enable both. It is always personally costly, so keep prayer central. Like Moses, we need to seek God's presence in everything we do (Exodus 33:14-15).

It is vital that the organisation is not dependent on one personality. Many charismatic and enthusiastic individuals start up projects and attract people to work with them. However, when that individual leaves for whatever reason, it can be difficult to "fill the void". In the excitement of starting up a team, and the day to day busyness of working with the women, it is unlikely that you will be thinking about what happens if the leader or founder leaves. However, every ministry is finite, and no one can continue for ever. You should be thinking about long term strategy and training people up who are able to take responsibility when the time comes.[38]

4. Volunteers

The ways in which people can contribute are endless – prayer, baking cakes, cooking meals, wrapping presents at Christmas, fundraising, speaking at awareness raising events, general administration, outreach, drop-in and befriending.

Introductory training before interviewing helps prospective volunteers have an idea of what they are letting themselves in for. Remember to ask for references. In some countries, security checks will be required. We recommend that "front line" volunteers (i.e. people who are going to be working directly with service users) be willing to sign up for an initial period of three years as it takes a long time to build up relationships with women who have attachment issues.

There are three main things to look for in volunteers:
- Love for God – a strong and resilient faith
- Self-awareness – a knowledge of personal strengths, weaknesses and wounds which may be exposed during ministry
- Teachability – openness to different perspectives, ability to listen to others, and willingness to learn new things

---

38. See Helen Sworn "How can we promote sustainability and succession in terms of vision, leadership and funding for the organisations we work with?" in *Finding our Way through the Traffick: Navigating the Complexities of a Christian Response to Sexual Exploitation and Trafficking* (eds) Christa Foster Crawford & Glenn Miles with Gundelina Veazco Eugene, OR: Wipf & Stock 2017, 12-18.

It is crucial that your volunteers feel honoured and valued as much as staff members; however, you need to be honest, too. If the team feels that a volunteer is turning into a liability then it is important that this is expressed, and that the person is helped to understand how they can improve their work. Sometimes obstructiveness can be a symptom of a deeper problem, as in the case of Angela, in the previous chapter.

It is essential to have a contract with volunteers to ensure that there is continuity and the working relationships and policies are clear. Volunteers should be fully aware of the policies of the organisation and adhere to them.

5. Governance and Fundraising

When you feel the time is right to start employing people, you need to take into account the laws of the country you are living in with regard to salary, taxation, insurance and so forth. You will need advice and accountability on these matters. Find older, experienced believers whom you respect and establish a Board of Trustees, according to the legal requirements in your setting. Here too, it is good to have people from diverse backgrounds who have a variety of gifts and expertise such as finance, legal knowledge, as well as theological and spiritual wisdom. Board members can be asked to review, monitor and assess specific programmes of action which you are proposing, and help you develop vision and plans for the future.

The Board of Trustees (or equivalent) is there to provide accountability for the organisation, but its primary role is to ensure that the project is adhering to its stated aims and objectives, in accordance with the law of the land. If your project becomes larger than expected then it might be time for you to consider charitable status, especially if you are receiving funding from other agencies and bodies. Find out what the law requires with regard to running charitable, non-profit organisations and adhere to it.

If appropriate, appoint a fundraiser – someone who is gifted in communicating the aims and ethos of your ministry, organising fundraising events and in liaising with grant-giving organisations. We recommend that you have diverse funding streams, so that you are not reliant on one single source of funding. A good rule of thumb is to have one third church, one third grants, and one third private individuals as your funding sources.

Keep reliance on God at the centre of your thinking. Fundraising is there to empower the work – not the other way around. Steer clear of donors who dictate how the money they give is spent – you may find yourself compromising your vision and ethos because the funder wants to call the shots. Don't change your vision to fit in with viable attractive funding options. Fundraising is important, but remember that some of the best ministries have no money at all.

Even at Board level, things may not be straightforward. When Lydia and Tom realised they needed to appoint Trustees to oversee their project and to comply with charity law, they selected people who were personally known to them, and who understood the vision. At first this worked well, but when they had to increase the number of Trustees, problems began. One person never attended the meetings and finally had to be removed. Another began to promote an agenda which did not align with the mission and ethos of the project. Another was always argumentative and did not seem to support the leadership. All this was counter-productive, frustrating and painful, and hindered the development and smooth running of the project for some time.

The controlling donor

6. Policies and Codes of Conduct

Devise policies which will ensure the smooth-running of the organisation and protect both team members and service users. Policies are simply agreed rules which should be followed and which come from experience, for example, "never go out on outreach alone – always work in pairs".

Topics to think about here include:
- Handling money
- Child protection (safeguarding)
- Data protection
- Recruitment
- Disciplinary procedures
- Staff appraisal
- Terms and conditions of employment
- Food handling
- Emergency procedures
- Health and safety
- Home visits – accompanied or unaccompanied?

It is essential to be sure that no member of staff or volunteer exploits the people you are working with – sexually, emotionally, financially, or physically. There has been enough exposure of abuse in church settings recently to make us aware that even if we might like to think such a thing could never happen in Christian circles, it certainly does. Christians are just as vulnerable to greed, lust and pride as anyone else, and if they deny that this is so, trouble will set in. For these reasons it is crucial that safeguarding measures are put in place. In some countries it is a statutory obligation to have each volunteer and staff member vetted to make sure they are not on the sex-offender register or have some other history of offending which should be taken into account in this type of work.

The safeguarding policies are as much for the protection of staff and volunteers as they are for the people you are working with. It is quite common for people to make accusations against those who are trying to help them, and you should take steps to ensure that everything is transparent and recorded. False accusations are highly distressing, bewildering and damaging for all concerned. Often these accusations are made out of spite, anger, fear, or confusion.

If the ministry is to survive and thrive, there must be an atmosphere of trust. This comes from the top down. The person at the top has to be completely trustworthy, and there must be no sense that they are "empire building" for themselves. There must also be trust between team members.

Be prepared continually to revise any written guidelines, policies or codes of conduct as you gain in experience – nothing should be set in stone.

7. Confidentiality and Data Protection

Besides the safeguarding policies mentioned above, it is essential to have a confidentiality policy. This will vary from culture to culture – some community-based cultures do not have the concept of privacy which is so important in the West. Nevertheless, it is crucial that those you meet and work with know that whatever they say to you will not be repeated to other people. Some basic guidelines are: Have a locked cupboard in which to keep notes and records. If you are keeping information on computers, it is essential to ensure that your record-keeping system complies with the data protection laws of your country. Who should have access to it? Are you keeping the material in your computers protected, or could it be accessible to outsiders? Have you taken adequate precautions against "hacking"? These are crucial questions which could make or break your project and it is vital that you get them right. Once again, take advice from people who know about these things in your setting.

Devise a system of written notes and information. Keep notes of meetings with women in a safe place. If the organisation becomes involved in an individual's care, ask the woman to fill in a background information form in which she gives her address, date of birth, and other personal details such as number of children and next of kin. All these documents are confidential (see below) but should be available for other team members to consult if they need to. In general, if a woman asks to see her notes, she has a right to do so. This does not apply, however, to letters sent to you by medical practitioners; these are strictly confidential and you should ask the permission of the doctor before anyone outside of the team sees it.

If a woman asks a team member if she is able to keep something she is told confidential, it should be explained to her that this depends on what she is going to say. There may be occasions when it is necessary to share something with another team member in order to get some advice on how to handle a situation. In some countries, there is a legal requirement to report cases of child abuse.

When you are writing prayer letters and publicity, or speaking about the work in churches, never use the women's real names – always use pseudonyms names and seek their permission to tell their story.

Devise a confidential notes system

8. Training

According to research amongst mission organisations, the more highly educated the team members, the more likely they are to stay.[39] However, this is a fact rather than a preference. Every believer has a talent, and should be encouraged to develop and use it. The first disciples were unschooled fishermen who became learners. We have a responsibility to enable believers to discover and cultivate their talents and use them for the glory of God (Matthew 25:15). The last thing we want is to find ourselves saying, "My people are destroyed from lack of knowledge" (Hosea 4:6).

If we look after our teams well, providing them with regular training opportunities and building up their skills, they will stay longer.

Encourage reading and have a resource library in your premises. Keep abreast of the latest thinking about the kinds of problems you are likely to come up against – for example, on addictions, attitudes to the sex industry or safeguarding policies.

---

39. Hay et al., *Worth Keeping*, 55.

Make regular team trainings and continuing professional development a priority. Bible study is an important component of team meetings and trainings. Ideas for training include

- basic listening skills
- first aid
- principles of mission
- health issues
- spirituality and prayer
- conflict resolution.

Training should be continuous and innovative, not sporadic and repetitive. It is good to link up with other teams and have training days together. Use the resources which have already been produced by other organisations. Theological colleges and established mission agencies can provide classes and good material.

9. Networking and Co-operation

In all ministry, it is very easy to become inward-looking and "precious", believing that we are the only ones doing this kind of work. It is more than likely that others have met the kind of problems you are facing and come up with strategies for dealing with them. We so often "reinvent the wheel", thinking that we have to do everything ourselves and forgetting that there are people who may have experiences and knowledge from which we can learn. The truth is that we all make enough mistakes of our own, so where possible it's best to take advice from those who have experience so that we do not make avoidable mistakes.

Networking is a way of meeting people who are involved in similar work to ourselves. Being part of various networks means that you can look for advice or information and share experiences. The crucial thing is to maintain our Christian identity and integrity.

If you find yourself wondering whether or not you should be working with a group which does not share your Christian values – say, a statutory body or a group of a different religion – ask yourself the question: would my refusal to work with this group help either to perpetuate risk, harm and danger for my client group or to hinder the development of services for them? Collaboration with non-Christian agencies offers another opportunity for others to see a different way of being and doing. Networking can also be across borders. International groups such as the International Christian Alliance on Prostitution (ICAP) can provide mutual assistance, information sharing, inspiration and training.[40]

40. *https://www.icapglobal.org*

BIBLE STUDY

Read Numbers 11: Moses feels the stresses of leadership.
We tend to want God to make our lives easy. We think that because we are doing his work things should be made as smooth and trouble free for us as possible. But God doesn't work that way. Moses had a challenging time leading his people, who were disobedient, distrustful and always grumbling. Even God's patience was tested, and Moses became so exhausted by the burden that at one point he declared that he wanted to die. God told him to appoint others who could share the load of responsibility with him, and so his strength was renewed.

QUESTIONS FOR DISCUSSION

> How did Moses deal with the stresses and strains of leadership?
> Why is it so important for leaders to learn to delegate and spread the burden of responsibility?
> How would you go about getting advice about financial, safeguarding and legal matters? Can you identify people who might be able to help you in these areas?
> How would you go about tackling the difficulties with a team member who disregards policies and procedures?

CHAPTER 8

Resilience in Ministry

They made me keeper of the vineyards; but my own vineyard I have not kept!

Songs of Songs 1:6 (ESV)

Do not think that love, in order to be genuine, has to be extraordinary. What we need is to love without getting tired.

Mother Theresa

1. The realities of ministry – Eleanor's experience

ELEANOR, A MIDDLE CLASS 22-year-old graduate, felt a call to work with commercially sexually exploited women. She was naïve and hadn't a clue what was involved – she just knew she wanted to do something to help the women she saw on the streets of her city. Fortunately, Eleanor hadn't made the same mistake as Andy and Emma. She had done some research and found a project which seemed to do the kind of work she wanted to be involved with. The project provided pre-selection training which helped her to see the realities of what she might be getting involved in and insisted that she go through a rigorous selection process.

Eleanor was accepted, and soon she found herself on the outreach team on Thursday nights. Week in week out, she would go out in the van, with the soup, tea and coffee, and meet the women. She got to know them, enjoyed meeting them for follow up in cafés, and came to love them. After a while, she came to realise just how precarious their lives were, and she became tired – why was there so much suffering and why was there so little change? Then, within a month, two women she knew well were found dead. Connie's death from an overdose was not unexpected – she had been becoming more reckless recently and had refused to take up a place in a residential drug rehabilitation centre when she was offered one. Nevertheless, her death was still a shock, and Eleanor couldn't help thinking that she could have done more to help her. Sally's death was a completely different matter. Eleanor had been meeting up with her regularly and had been with her on the day that she died. She had met her in a café and had read the Bible with her. Sally, Eleanor reported to the team that evening, had begun to accept the fact that God loved her and might even like her too. The next morning, Sally's body was found in a rubbish bin. She had been stabbed seventeen times and strangled. Beside her was found a handbag containing a Bible and a notebook in which Eleanor had written, telling her how much God loved her. The police thought that Sally had been killed because she owed her drug dealer £15.

After Sally's death, Eleanor began to wonder if she was cut out for this kind of work. Not only was she physically and emotionally exhausted, her faith was challenged too. Could she have done more for Connie? Could she have taken her back to rehab the night she showed up at the drop-in? Why did God take Sally, just when she was beginning to see that she was loved? And why did her death have to be so brutal? It all seemed so meaningless.

I can't do this

Eleanor's story is a common one. The relentless, extreme suffering which frontline workers encounter means that many people struggle and there is a high drop-out rate. They start off with great enthusiasm and idealism but are soon overwhelmed by the needs that confront them and become discouraged when they encounter violence and extreme suffering or if they do not see "results" as quickly as they thought they would. How can we help people to persevere and be reliable, consistent and credible presences in the women's lives?

2. Looking after yourself

It is God's will that we should be His hands and feet, that we should love those involved in commercial sexual exploitation as Jesus does. However, the work is difficult and demanding. Many people start out with enthusiasm but find that the challenges are simply too great. The extreme suffering and stark injustices which they encounter can challenge everything they thought they knew and understood. Effective ministry in such an environment requires perseverance. But how can we do this without harming ourselves in the process? The attrition rate amongst frontline workers is high, and burnout common. Self-sacrifice is demanded of us and, as Paul says, believers are asked to share in Christ's sufferings (Phil 3:10; Romans

8:17). However, we need to be able to sustain ministry, bringing Christ's light into darkness consistently rather than sporadically, so self-care is vital.

In Christian culture it is often implicitly (and sometimes explicitly) taught that work is more important than anything else. Although most of us would say that we know this is not true, many of us slip into patterns of overwork which are ultimately counter-productive. But we need to be careful. Crowded diaries can make us feel important and wanted. They can give a sense of short-term fulfilment, a gratifying feeling of being needed. In the long term, however, we can become blind to what is really going on within ourselves and suffer burnout. It is easy to forget that our first calling is to focus on God rather than always to be doing something. We can become so intent on helping others that we fail to see that we are harming ourselves, or that we are actually trying to escape our own pain.

Human beings have a great capacity for self-deception. It can be easy to see when other people are falling into the trap of too much busyness, but hard to see it in ourselves. We can be unaware of, or intentionally blind to, our own overworking. This can be a response to a burden of shame, sense of inadequacy, fragile self-esteem or loneliness. We might be ignoring or disregarding problems in our home life or thinking that we are indispensable. We need to ask God to remove these "logs" from our own eyes (Luke 6:41-42) and help us to see clearly what is driving us. We should be active, but not hyper-active.

Some stress is necessary for us to function well, but if there is too much and for too long, burnout can be the result. Signs of burnout include:

- exhaustion and fatigue,
- a reduced sense of being able to cope
- cynicism (a distrust of people's motives)
- pessimism
- inability to relax
- irritability
- sleep disturbance.[41]

If you find some of these creeping into your life, it may be that you have had too much stress for too long, or that you have taken on too much. You may not recognise that there is anything wrong. Sometimes it is up to a line manager or team leader to see what is happening and step in. They might have to insist that a front-line worker prioritise family and friends in their lives rather than work. But there are steps that you can take to avoid burnout.

---

41. Andrew and Elizabeth Proctor *The Essential Guide to Burnout: Overcoming Excess Stress* Oxford: Lion Hudson 2013.

Ask yourself these questions and be honest in your answers: Am I too busy? If so, is this because I am trying to escape something in myself or my life? Or because I am unable to prioritise? Or because I am feeding a need to be needed? Am I trying to do things for which I am not gifted? Talk these things through honestly and openly with your mentor. Reflect on how you are feeling about the acute needs you see every day in commercial sexual exploitation. If you are struggling, don't be afraid to admit it. If you find that a role no longer energises you, but rather seems to leave you feeling depleted and joyless, it may be time to stop, take stock, and consider if there are other ways you can be contributing.

Feeling stressed? You need to talk!

Follow the command to take Sabbath (Exodus 20:8). We all have a tendency to allow our own human endeavours to take priority over our relationship with God. The command reminds us that our priority is to focus on God. If we take regular rest, we are more likely to be able to sustain long-term helping relationships in a highly stressful environment. If we work without taking physical and spiritual rest we will not only become exhausted and ill, we will lose perspective on our own place in God's scheme of things – we may start to think we are invincible and indispensable.

The command to keep Sabbath is not a matter of having one particular day off which must be kept at all costs, but rather a command to rest. So, it is important that we create space for ourselves and time to withdraw – anywhere as long as we can't be reached.

We also need to stay connected with supportive friends and family, and with our church communities. It is crucial that we maintain friendships in which "God reassurances" are the norm. Daily time with God and meeting with safe prayer partners should be a priority. We matter to God, who knows the number of hairs on our head (Matthew 10:30).

Learn to say "no". A frontline worker who can do this, even when there seems to be an urgent need, is a gift to any ministry. As one worker said, "I have to say no. If I can't say no, then soon I will need to say 'Sorry, I can't help you because I'm exhausted." There will always be crises in the women's lives, there will always be urgent needs. As you gain experience, you will build up a sense of when to respond and when to let things be, when to do things yourself and when to allow others to step in. You cannot (and should not) be available all the time as this will only encourage dependency. There will always be hospital visits to attend to, appointments at homeless units to keep, phone calls to be made, reports to be written. It need not always be you who deals with these things – your colleagues are just as capable of dealing with them as you are.

Give attention to your own personal and professional development. Take courses in topics such as communication, conflict resolution, and spirituality, interpersonal and ministry-related skills. Courses don't just keep you up to date with current thinking, they are also excellent opportunities for meeting new people, and getting out of the "bubble" of your own ministry for a while.

Develop a realistic view of your own strengths and weaknesses, and don't be afraid of making mistakes, for we can learn from them. Don't compare yourself with others – this will only undermine your confidence, or worse, cause jealousy and envy which ultimately damage relationships and destroy ministry. The letter of James puts it this way: "Where you have envy and selfish ambition, there you find disorder and every evil practice" (James 3:16). You have your own unique gifts and identity in Christ.

Be realistic about personal responsibility. Eleanor wondered if she could have done more to get Connie into rehab – but the truth is that we cannot make someone do something they don't want to do or protect them from every danger. As Psalm 49:7 says, "No one can redeem the life of another or give to God a ransom for them."

3. Trauma, Secondary Trauma and Compassion Fatigue

The world of commercial sexual exploitation is full of violence. Team members can find themselves involved in frightening situations which have a lasting impact, as Lydia found out. One day, she went to pick up a woman (Tilly) to take her to a Christian residential rehabilitation centre. Lydia didn't know that the flat she went to belonged to Tilly's pimp/perpetrator, whom we will call Frank. When Frank opened the door, Lydia saw that he had a gun. He let her in, keeping the gun pointed at her head. Then Lydia's phone rang. It was Tilly's Mum, who proceeded angrily to tell Lydia that she should not be wasting the project's money on sending Tilly to rehab, because she was "a f****** waste of space". Tilly's Mum ranted on for a few minutes, and when she had finished, Lydia, who was given a supernatural ability to remain calm in this terrifying situation, began to tell her that Tilly was made in the image of God and was beautiful and precious. Frank, who was listening all the while, put the gun down and eventually allowed Tilly to leave. Lydia took

Tilly to the rehab centre. At the time, Lydia had no sense of the incident having an effect on her, although she did ask God to help her see if anything was "broken" within her and where to access healing. A few weeks later, when she was going into another flat to conduct a Bible study with some of the women, she suddenly felt fear for no reason. She realised that the incident had left its mark and knew that she needed help to process the experience.

Lydia's experience illustrates just what a dangerous world we are entering when we become involved in this kind of ministry. She had experienced severe trauma, and later realised that she needed professional help to process what had happened. Her board of trustees realised that they should pay for specialised therapy for her as part of their staff care policy. We will have more to say about trauma in the chapter on mental health, but in the meantime we need to say that should you have experience of trauma like this, it is crucial that you receive psychological help in order to help you work through the experience and prevent PTSD.

At Gunpoint

In the course of your ministry you will hear many troubling, upsetting stories which may stay with you, and you may find yourself thinking about them over and over again. If you find yourself inordinately troubled, experiencing an intense sense of horror, fear and nightmares as a result of what you hear from others, you may be suffering from secondary trauma. If you find yourself listening to many such stories of suffering, you could find yourself less able to respond compassionately. This is known as compassion fatigue, in which you feel as if you just don't care anymore.

There is no such thing as total protection against being affected by what you hear. And there is no shame in finding that it is all becoming overwhelming. You can, however, help guard yourself. Awareness of the risks of over identifying with the women we work with, of thinking that we are the only ones who can help them, can help prevent secondary trauma. Sharing the load of listening with others on the team, and talking about your own reactions to what you are hearing and experiencing, is also important. You can do this, to a certain extent, in the debrief at the end of a ministry session but you should also find someone with whom you can share without breaking confidentiality and explore your responses to what you are hearing. This might be your prayer accountability partners, your pastor, therapist or mentor, or someone with good listening skills, who has experience of working with vulnerable adults. Making yourself accountable in this way will help you to keep things in proportion, protect you from overidentifying with the people you are working with and maintain a healthy balance between caring for people and being able to live your own life.

It is increasingly recognised that psychosocial support is imperative for those who experience extreme trauma and those who reach out to deeply traumatised people. As we have seen, Lydia was able to have independent, confidential therapy, paid for by her organisation. Full time workers should also have regular supervision. A good supervisor, whom you meet every six weeks or so, will help you reflect on what you are doing and provide psychological support. Good supervision helps build up resilience – helping with stress management, dealing with emotional reactions to events and debriefing after events such as the death of someone you have been working closely with. Your priority as the supervisee is to focus on learning, problem solving and choosing your own goals for development.

You will find that there is a constant need to learn and re-learn the balance between support and growth in ministry. Your support group and mentor's role is to help you in this task.

Good supervision helps build resilience

4. Spiritual health

Quite simply, you cannot do this kind of work without prayer. You have a responsibility to tend and cultivate your own spiritual life. The spiritual battle which this type of work involves should not be underestimated. Because of this, we cannot stress enough the importance of maintaining your own spiritual health, through worship, prayer, fellowship and Bible study. So, find your own best way of praying and be disciplined. Different people find different things work for them – you may find that going on a retreat regularly is helpful, or going to conferences and regular Bible studies or prayer meetings. Most important is to be part of a church community.

It is possible to be around darkness so much that it begins to distort our thinking. For example, behaviour we know to be wrong can become "normalised" and appear to be acceptable. We need to keep our spiritual life active in order to help us be able to keep our moral compass and to be able to sense when things are not right.

We are commanded to pray for ourselves and others. Sometimes, however, we can feel that our prayers go unheard, or that God refuses to answer our prayers. This can be hard to understand and be a real challenge to faith. Here it is helpful to remember four things. First, God does not treat His people as robots. In His perfect love He does not control us but allows us freedom to make mistakes so that we can learn from them. Second, if we never had tough experiences, we would never mature or develop resilience. James 1:12 puts it this way:

> "Blessed is the one who perseveres under trial because, having stood the test, that person will receive the crown of life that the Lord has promised to those who love him."

As we persevere in difficulties, we grow in strength and maturity. Third, as the Apostle Paul found out, God does not answer every prayer as we would desire. But Paul realised that his "thorn in the flesh" had a particular function – to keep him humble before God (2 Corinthians 12:6-7). Lastly, God can and does redeem situations and use them for his glory – even those situations which seem terrible to us. Joseph suffered terribly at the hands of his brothers, who sold him into slavery. In the end, however, he was able to see how God could bring good out of his brothers' evil intentions (Genesis 50:20).

The sheer depth of suffering which involvement in commercial sexual exploitation brings about can cause us to lose hope. When we are surrounded by insurmountable needs we can begin to think that things will never change and that there is nothing we can do. We might be tempted to give up. We might even stop praying. If this happens, remember Christ's command to go and make disciples of all the nations (Matthew 28:19-20). Believers do not have an option in this: it is a matter of obedience, and if we are obedient, we are going some way to keeping hope alive. Remember Paul's teaching that it is when we feel at our weakest that we are actually at our strongest, for that is when we stop relying on our own resources and rely on God himself (2 Cor 12:8-10). This is when hope can begin to be re-kindled, because when we are at the end of ourselves, God steps in. Even if we find ourselves finding it difficult to pray, Jesus himself is interceding for us (Romans 8:34).

Learn to have a healthy attitude towards death. Women who are involved in commercial sexual exploitation are at a far greater risk of being murdered, or of dying young from disease or injury, than other members of the public. There is no doubt that we will lose people we have become fond of. It can be bewildering, for example, to lose someone we have invested in, prayed for and got to know well.

Like Eleanor, many workers find the deaths of women hard to understand and to tolerate, but it is possible for us to forget that in Christian perspective, in God's mercy, death might be the better thing, bringing peace and release from suffering. We may feel that we are going through hell on earth as we witness terrible injustice and suffering, but the promise of Scripture is that one day God will bring an end to suffering and establish a new order:

> "He will wipe every tear from their eyes. There will be no more death or mourning or crying or pain, for the old order of things has passed away" (Revelation 21:4)

Be real. In some Christian circles it is considered dangerous and even sinful to express doubt and anger against God. We are often told that we should not cause other believers to stumble and that we should always be positive and upbeat about our faith. In the end, though, this approach can lead us into spiritual trouble – for we are not being honest. Working in the area of commercial sexual exploitation will lead you to ask questions, and to doubt. This is healthy. It is healthy to have questions – to wonder why some women are able to leave commercial sexual exploitation while others remain trapped. It is healthy to shout at God when a woman you have got to know and love is murdered. It is far better to be honest about our disappointments and anger with God than to pretend that nothing is wrong. There is good precedent for this in the prophets and Psalms and we can use their words in our own prayers. Here, for example, are the protests of Habakkuk:

> "How long, Lord, must I call for help,
> but you do not listen?
> Or cry out to you, 'Violence!'
> But you do not save? Why do you make me look at injustice?
> Why do you tolerate wrongdoing?
> Destruction and violence are before me;
> there is strife, and conflict abounds.
> Therefore, the law is paralysed, and justice never prevails.
> The wicked hem in the righteous,
> so that justice is perverted." (Habakkuk 1:2-4)

Honest questioning is a far better basis of faith, a far more attractive kind of spirituality than denial and suppressed anger which will only express itself in other ways which put people off rather than bring them to God. Sometimes we are asked where God is in all this. It is better simply to say "I don't know" than provide facile answers. Ultimately, it is only God who knows the answers, and we have to ask for grace and peace in the midst of all the complexities and questions.

Sometimes, becoming involved in ministry can bring things to light in ourselves. Lily, who joined the same team as Eleanor, had been praying for years to understand why she had difficulty trusting authority figures. During her volunteer training, she realised for the first time that this stemmed from the sexual abuse her step-father had inflicted on her when she was a child. Now God answered her prayer and she was finally able to identify the cause of the deep unnamed emotional pain she had been carrying. Lily became a key team member and developed a vital ministry of praying for others with similar experiences to hers. God was able to redeem Lily's experience and use them for his healing purposes.

5. Following up…

Eleanor did stay on in the end – much to her own and others' surprise. Her prayer partners and mentor helped her to think through her experiences and find peace. She also began to look at her own past experiences of abuse (memories she had long tried to avoid) and sought counselling herself. She made sure she took time off and benefitted from reflective learning and on-going training. So Eleanor grew in self-awareness. Of course, trouble did not go away. There were other times of crisis with the women, and there were personality clashes and theological disagreements in the team. She also had to wrestle with the mystery of unanswered prayer, to learn that God knows and loves people far more than we ever can and to trust in his goodness. Somehow, she was able to be keep perspective and came to be regarded as a wise resource by the other team members.

BIBLE STUDY

Read Hebrews 12:1-3 Some Good Advice

The author of the letter to the Hebrews was writing to people who were undergoing or at risk of experiencing persecution, but the principles he outlines can be applied to any kind of trial or task in which we are likely to endure opposition. He speaks first of all of self-awareness – we need self-awareness in order to be able to recognise when and what we need to "throw off", and honesty with ourselves to admit it. We also need help to run the race – we cannot do this ourselves. Above all, the key to all endurance was to fix our eyes on Jesus, "the author and perfecter of our faith".

QUESTIONS FOR DISCUSSION

> Do you find it easy or hard to rest and keep Sabbath? What can you do to make more of a balance between ministry and rest?

> "Better a handful of quietness than two hands full of toil and chasing after the wind." Ecclesiastes 4:6." What strategies do you have, or can you develop, to find space and silence in your schedule?

> Have you any experience of disharmony amongst teams? How was it resolved and what were the long-term consequences? What did you learn which would enable you to prevent disunity in the future?

> How can you encourage self-awareness and accountability amongst your team members?

> How would you support someone who faces a struggle like Eleanor's? What strategies has your team put in place for supporting team members at times like this?

CHAPTER 9

Exploitation, Abuse and Violence

"Though I cry, "Violence!" I get no response; though I call for help, I get no justice"

Job 19:7

"My God, my God, why have you forsaken me?"

Matthew 27:46

1. Alice's Story

ONE EVENING, WHEN Tom and Lydia were on outreach, Alice decided to talk. She told of the night she had been walking along the street when a well-dressed man drew up beside her in a Mercedes. He jumped out of the car and pushed her into an alleyway. Stinking of alcohol, he pulled down her trousers and forced a metal rod into her vagina, drawing blood. Then he threw her violently against a lamp post and left. All the time he said nothing – he just attacked her and drove off. However, Alice realised she knew him – he was a respectable local businessman. But she didn't report the incident, she just went on working as if nothing had happened. Now she was talking about it for the first time, and she couldn't recall when it had taken place. All she could remember was that it had been cold, so it must have been winter.

The car drew up beside her

Tom and Lydia were shocked at her story, but they were even more distressed by the realisation that violence of this sort was nothing new for Alice. She had been brought up by foster carers because her Mum, who was an alcoholic, had broken her arm when she was eight years old. Two boys in the foster family sexually abused her for several years until she ran away at 15. During this time of child sexual abuse, Alice received nothing, financial or otherwise, from her abusers. But after she ran away, and discovered that she could make money selling sex, she felt empowered. Then one night, after she was gang raped, heroin proved to be a powerful emotional painkiller, and she was able to carry on working. She and her "boyfriend", Seb, were together for a long time and they had two children who were taken into care. Alice reckoned she probably deserved it when Seb beat her- especially when she didn't bring in enough money.

2. Child Sexual Abuse and Exploitation

Commercial sexual exploitation is saturated in violence. In 2003, research carried out in nine countries revealed the extent of violence which women in commercial exploitation have to endure: out of 854 people interviewed, 71% had been physically assaulted and 63% had been raped.[42] A study carried out in the United States in 2004 estimated that female sex workers are 18 times more likely to be murdered than women in the general population.[43]

Many victims of commercial sexual exploitation have grown up in families in which violence and abuse was the norm. They may also have been subject to sexual abuse, by family members or friends, or authority figures. Abuse which takes place within families, or is perpetrated by family friends, tends to breed secrecy and remains hidden. Abusers devise ways for victims to feel pleasure and so feel complicit in the abuse, which leads to self-loathing and compounds shame. For the victim, disclosing what has happened to them can feel acutely dis-honouring to their family. Some fear that it will damage family members if the truth becomes known – "If I told my Mum what my father had done to me, she would believe me and her whole life would fall apart". The desire to honour the family clashes with the need for honest disclosure which is needed for healing.

The effects of the trauma last well into adulthood – emotional instability, depression, and PTSD are common. Victims are also at greater risk of sexual exploitation. They may also become caught in unwanted sexual behaviour such as sex-buying

---

42. Farley, M., Cotton, A., Lynne, J., Zumbeck, S., Spiwak, F., Reyes, M., Alvarez, D. and Sezgin, U. (2003). "Prostitution and Trafficking in Nine Countries: An Update on Violence and Posttraumatic Stress Disorder" in Melissa Farley (ed) *Prostitution, Trafficking and Traumatic Stress* Binghampton: Haworth Press 2003, 33-74.

43. Potterat, J. J., Brewer, D. D., Muth, S. Q., Rothenberg, R. B., Woodhouse, D. E., Muth, J. B., Stites, H., Brody, S. (2004). "Mortality in a Long-Term Open Cohort of Prostitute Women" American Journal of Epidemiology 159, 778-785 (782).

and pornography addiction, which could contribute to the perpetuation of violence in commercial sexual exploitation. As Jay Stringer notes, "You are far more likely to be seduced into recreating the dynamic of your sexual abuse than into the mere pursuit of sexual pleasure."[44]

Child Sexual Exploitation (CSE) is a form of sexual abuse in which a child or young person who is under the age of consent is manipulated or forced into taking part in a sexual act.[45] Both boys and girls are affected. Children are manipulated and often groomed to be used by individuals or gangs, or for work in prostitution. Groomers present themselves as the "saviour" from neglect, boredom and harm. Victims become isolated from friends and family; sometimes their exploiters drug them. They may be moved around the country in which they live, or taken abroad, in order to provide buyers with sexual services. Or they may have come from areas of extreme poverty (for example, street children) in which submitting to sexual exploitation or prostitution was the only way to survive.

Children can be groomed on-line for purposes of sexual exploitation. Adults pretend that they are children and befriend their victims in online chat rooms and social media websites. Sexual exploitation need not only be actual sexual contact – children may be forced to take part in sexualised conversations on the telephone or to be photographed in sexualised situations on-line (cybersex trafficking).

All children are at risk from sexual exploitation, grooming and pimping. Nevertheless, certain groups seem to be at more risk than others. Alice and Jody (whom we met in chapter 1) were targeted when they left residential or foster care. Involvement in gangs also puts children at risk of exploitation and abuse. Unaccompanied children who are migrants or asylum seekers are also very much at risk. Children who come from unstable backgrounds and who have a deep need for love and security may be tricked into thinking that they are safe with perpetrators who ultimately only want to use them for their own purposes. If a child has already been abused sexually by an adult, the risk of exploitation is increased – they may believe that to be treated in this way is the norm. Some important signs point towards the possibility that a child is being sexually exploited:

- They are missing school regularly
- They are out at nights and come home very late
- They are defensive and secretive about what they are doing

44. Stringer *Unwanted* Kindle Location 75

45. The age of consent, which is the legal age at which an individual is considered mature enough to consent to sex, differs from country to country. For example, in the United Kingdom and Russia it is 16, in Brazil and Myanmar it is 14, 13 in Japan, 12 in the Philippines and in Nigeria it is 11. In America it varies from state to state (16-18 years). Some countries (e.g. Sudan, Saudi Arabia and Yemen) have no minimum age of consent but insist that sexual relationships take place only within marriage.

- They have unexplained possessions, e.g. money or mobile phones
- They have a sexually transmitted disease
- They have mood swings or cry easily
- They behave in an inappropriately sexualised way.
- They are secretive and withdrawn
- They look tired or unwell
- They are taking drugs or alcohol
- There are marks on their bodies which they try to hide
- They self-harm or have suicidal tendencies

People who sexually exploit children are committing a crime. It is important that you know and understand the law as to what you should do if you suspect that a child is being physically abused or sexually exploited. If you are in a country in which you are required by law to report suspected abused or exploitation then you must comply with this, and your agency must keep good records of your interactions with children.

3. Violence in commercial sexual exploitation

Alice's story illustrates the complex nature of violence in commercial sexual exploitation. In the eyes of most sex buyers, Alice is simply a body to be hired for a while. In their view, by accepting payment she has given implicit "consent" to fulfilling their desires, and they can do whatever they want with her. Her wishes and preferences are irrelevant, and if she does not please the customers, it is their right to do something about it. This is why violence and rape are so much a part of the women's experience. Mia de Faoite explains:

Know the signs of Child Sexual Exploitation

> "You know when you buy something and it doesn't work properly, the first thing you will do is pick it up and shake it. The same principle applies to prostitution. If your mouth isn't open wide enough or your throat isn't deep

enough (*Sic*). So you are always at risk of being raped or abused if the buyer feels he is not getting what he paid for."

De Faoite notes the link between sex buying and power – they are buying power over a woman's body. Violence will keep her compliant. "You must ask yourself, what are they buying? It's power. It's a very powerful thing to have control of somebody's body in that way. It's a power fix and they know it." [46]

Sex buyers may compel a woman to engage in sexual acts to which she has not agreed. They may abuse her by tying her up, beating her, urinating or defecating on her. Rape is common, including with objects such as bottles. Or she may be taken to a secluded location and raped by several men, while the buyer watches. Often, in these situations, no payment is given. Sometimes, the view that women in prostitution are worthless and contemptible results in the kind of random attack that Alice experienced that night on the streets. The attacker saw an opportunity to vent his anger and hurt someone with impunity– for who would believe her story? The testimony of a drug addicted woman in prostitution would be nothing compared to that of a respected local businessman.

But violence is not only inflicted by men. Every so often, women take it out on each other. Tom and Lydia were stunned one night when Zoë came into the drop in, took off her top and showed them the scar she received from another woman called Imogen. They had been in competition for business in a crack house, and Zoë had been chosen rather than Imogen. Imogen had recently been beaten up for not giving all her earnings to her "partner", and when Zoë got the work and she didn't, she went for her with a knife. Imogen felt no remorse, and Zoë expressed no anger – it was just business. Violence amongst women can arise when there is competition for custom, or if money is needed for drugs, or from female pimps/perpetrators who are trying to keep control. In an environment in which women so often look out for and protect each other, lines become blurred and sometimes it is the survival of the fittest.

And sometimes, women attack sex buyers. It is not uncommon for the police to receive reports of violence perpetrated by women against sex buyers. By humiliating them and hurting them they can take revenge for their own childhood victimisation and suffering.

4. Power, Coercion and Control

Victims of commercial sexual exploitation are kept under control by means of physical and sexual violence. Another way of inflicting physical violence is to

---

46. Quoted in Sophie Walker "Let's Criminalise the men buying sex, and spare the women they exploit" *The Guardian* Monday 21st May 2018. For more on the violence of commercial sexual exploitation, see Kathleen Barry *The Prostitution of Sexuality* New York: New York University Press 1995.

withhold drugs or alcohol when someone is addicted, or to provide too much. Sexual violence could include forcing a woman to have unprotected sex, or filming her against her will. But pimps/perpetrators or partners use other means too, as the diagram shows. He might exercise "male privilege" – denying her any say in the relationship, making sure she knows who is boss. He might tell her what to wear, and when she will go out to work. [47] Isolation is another tactic. When Esther (chapter 5) met the team that first night and was given a cupcake, her pimp made sure she never saw them again. She wasn't allowed to make any friends, and he controlled what she watched on TV. He took all her money (economic abuse). He told her that she was worthless and nothing but a "slut, nothing but a whore", and "only good for one thing" (emotional abuse). Just as she was getting used to a town, he would move her to another one, refusing to allow her to go to drop-in centres or other services (isolation). Although she spent every night walking up and down the street, she was in a bubble – too afraid to talk to anybody outside her exploitative community and seek an alternative to the 'hell on earth' in which she was trapped.

Besides beating her, Seb would use other tactics to keep Alice under control. Alice threatened to leave him but he told her it would be her fault if

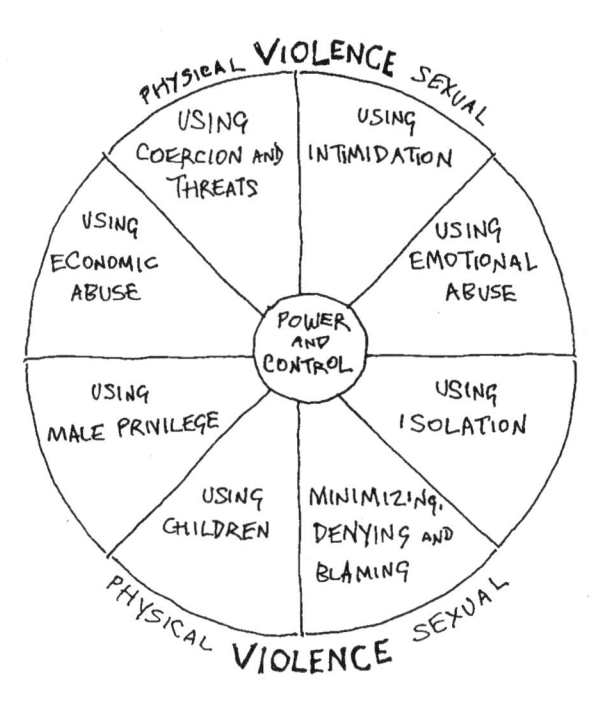

Cycle of power and control

he committed suicide, so she stayed. When he was drunk, he would smash things in the house (coercion, threats, intimidation). But, despite the beatings Alice felt that Seb really loved her because he brought her everything she needed, looked out for her when she was working, and got her the drugs she needed (encouraging alcohol and drug dependence). He sometimes even brought her presents.

Alice has become unable to discern the difference between what is abuse and what is not. She is an object in an unequal power game, and she cannot see it. When customers hurt her, or when she complains about Seb's beatings, he tells her

---

47. Here we are drawing on the Duluth Model as used by the Domestic Abuse Intervention Programme https://www.theduluthmodel.org/what-is-the-duluth-model/ accessed December 30th 2019.

she deserves everything she gets (<u>stigmatising, undermining, blaming</u>) if she doesn't do her job properly. Seb's tactics are designed to wear her down, confuse her and reduce her resolve to care for herself, thus keeping her completely dependent on him and under his control.

Emotional and psychological abuse also comes from sex buyers. In fact, continuous "servicing" of sex buyers, perhaps up to twenty or thirty a day, is itself psychologically damaging, as the woman's sense of personhood is eroded. She is merely an object to be used, not a human being to be respected and honoured. Sex buyers can and do force women to name themselves in degrading terms, as "slut", "whore", and much worse. They may insist that women engage in humiliating conversations and sex acts, such as dressing up in school uniform or pretending to be a relative of the client – remember "Uncle Andrew" in chapter 1? Sex buyers can also refuse to pay (these are known as "clippers") or demand more for their money, make her do things she abhors.

5. How can we help?

The effects of violence and exploitation in a woman's life are profound and long-lasting – physically, emotionally, and spiritually. Women will carry physical wounds, which may cause problems years after the event. All have been subjected to severe trauma. The study carried out in 2003 by Melissa Farley and her team discovered that 68% of the women they had interviewed met the criteria for PTSD (see chapter 11). But like Alice, they can become immune to the effects of violence and coercion, seeing it as normal and inevitable. If they have been subjected to violence as a child, the sense of normality and inevitability is increased. A common result of this cycle is "mental defeat" in which a woman gives up any idea of being able to do

He sometimes bought her presents

anything for herself, unable to resist her abuser, and even any idea of being an individual in her own right.[48]

Many women feel too afraid to report the violence to the police, or they may feel that there is no point if the police are corrupt, as is the case in many countries. One night, Nell's friend Mala managed to escape from the brothel in Thailand in which they both lived and ran to the police station. However, one of the police officers, who was being bribed by the madam to keep the brothel open, took her back there. Mala realised that she couldn't trust anyone – especially those in authority.

Our role in ministry is to provide a safe place in which to explore feelings and fears; we can help women identify and voice experiences which they may not have done before. This might mean giving time to listen or making a referral to specialist counselling services if these are available. We can create an atmosphere of peace and calm and model relationships which are not characterised by violence. In certain circumstances, it may be helpful to have a couple of male volunteers who can demonstrate respectful relationships with the women.

It may be helpful to hold a meeting or workshop in which women discuss strategies to avoid violent situations. Women are more likely to learn from each other than from people who have no personal experience. You could, for example, discuss these tips for keeping safe, and encourage women to come up with some of their own:

- Always work in pairs
- Note down vehicle registration numbers
- Work only in designated areas
- Don't work while drunk

Find out if there are agencies which deal with violence against women and domestic abuse and use their resources with the women. Small group discussions can enable women to share their experiences in a safe environment. If you suspect that the woman might be suffering from PTSD, encourage her to get medical help.

Bible studies are useful ways of encouraging women to talk about their experiences. The story of Tamar, for example, which we have included below, tells of an example of rape and incest. Encourage the women to discuss the passage from their perspective – you may be surprised by their insights. The story of the Samaritan woman at the well can be used to talk about how Jesus relates to women (John 4:4-26). Also of use are passages from the prophets which emphasise God's heart for the poor and oppressed, such as Isaiah 61:1 and Amos 5:2. If the women agree, offer to pray with them and encourage them to pray themselves.

---

48. Ehlers, A. A. Maercker & A. Boos "Post Traumatic Stress Disorder following political imprisonment: the role of mental defeat, alienation and perceived permanent change" Journal of Abnormal Psychology 109 (2000), 45-55.

But we can do much more. Giving the women rape alarms helps teach the women that violence should not be considered an occupational hazard and is never to be tolerated. It helps get the message across that each one matters and has a right to live without fear of violence. We can encourage local initiatives to help reduce the risk of violent attack on victims of commercial sexual exploitation. Of course, this will depend on your setting and the willingness and capabilities of the authorities. But it can be very effective to become involved in local policy-making. For example, some groups have campaigned for designated areas in which the women are monitored by plain clothes police in unmarked cars, and with CCTV surveillance. Initiatives like these can be very effective in reducing the numbers of assaults on women as they work.

Lastly, just as we can examine our own attitudes towards money and wealth, we can also address the causes of gender-based violence which is so much a part of commercial sexual exploitation. As Lori Heise writes,

> "Violence against women and girls is not just about individually violent men. It is a much larger systemic issue. Violence is caused by gender inequality and related to ideas about men needing to be strong and in control. To stop violence against women, we need to change the norms and structural gender inequalities in society."[49]

Where there is a belief that men are superior to women, gender-based violence will be found. No Christian would condone female genital mutilation, rape as a weapon of war, or selective abortion (for example). But many Christian communities do limit the roles and opportunities that women can have in society, prohibiting them from having a voice – all on the basis that women are inferior to men. These ideas can become so ingrained in a culture that women themselves can come to believe that this is the right and proper order of things which should not be changed – and it can subtly lead to the belief that violence against women is acceptable. But Christians are called to take the side of the oppressed; we can call out injustice of this sort when we see it. We can also make sure that our communities embody the equality between men and women which being made in the image of God entails.

---

49. Lori Heise "The Conversation" December 10, 2014 http://theconversation.com/to-stop-violence-against-women-we-need-to-get-men-to-help-change-social-norms-35265 (accessed 4th March 2019).

BIBLE STUDY

Read 2 Samuel 13:1-22

The story of Amnon and Tamar

This story is a harrowing example of gender-based violence. Tamar is a prime example of the "objectification of women" – she is viewed as an object by Amnon, something that he can use for his own pleasure and gratification. Amnon decides that he is going to have sex with her and makes sure he gets what he wants by exerting force. The cultural climate is one in which this can be aided and abetted – Tamar has to do what she is told – she must go and prepare food for him, whether she wants to or not. Simply because she is a woman, Tamar must comply. When the rape happens, her protests and cries go unheeded. Even her expression of grief after the rape is an act of courage, however, as she will likely become an object of shame in the family – as David's reaction suggests.

QUESTIONS FOR DISCUSSION

> Discuss what steps you and your team should take if you suspect that a child is being sexually exploited.
> How are women viewed in your culture? What aspects of it do you think are likely to promote gender-based violence?
> According to Galatians 3:28, in Christ Jesus there is neither Jew nor Greek, slave or free, male or female. How far do you think this statement is taken seriously in your church community?
> Amnon is said to have hated Tamar after he raped her – why?
> If Alice came to your drop-in, how would you help her?
> Christians are called to be "speak up for those who cannot speak for themselves" (Proverbs 31: 8-9). In what ways can you speak out against violence and exploitation?

CHAPTER 10

Health and Illness

"I was ill and you looked after me...."

Matt 25:36

1. Introduction

WHEN DIANE FIRST arrived at the drop-in, the team was shocked at her appearance. She was terribly thin, and her teeth were in very poor condition. She had extensive bruising, dark circles under her eyes, and seemed exhausted. Lydia got her a warm drink and something to eat, and sat and chatted with her for a while. The bruising, she learned, was from a recent encounter with a sex buyer who had beaten Diane up and left her at the side of the road. Lydia soon realised, however, that there was something else going on – for Diane was running a fever. Alarmed at how weak and tired she was, Tom and Lydia tried to get her to see a doctor, but Diane wasn't keen, insisting that she felt "fine", and that she just needed a couple of hours rest.

There are many health risks associated with commercial sexual exploitation. The more clients a woman has, the more likely she is to become infected with anything from the common cold to the HIV virus, and to be injured as a result of assault. The risks increase if there is drug or alcohol abuse. This chapter aims to provide

Discussing health issues

you with general information about major health problems you might encounter and to enable you to help the women minimise the risks and consequences of serious illness. It will also give you some tips on how to help people through illness.

Some women, like Diane, will be reluctant to seek medical help, perhaps out of fear of what might be discovered, or perhaps because they see the doctor as an unwelcome authority figure. Others may be too ashamed to go to the doctor, not wanting it to be known that they are working in prostitution. For many, medical treatment will be beyond their financial means. In some inner-city areas, clinics and drop-in centres are provided specifically for sex workers. If there is one in your area, get to know the staff and encourage the women to use the services provided there.

2. Physical Problems

Promiscuity brings with it increased risks of sexual and reproductive health problems. Women in prostitution are vulnerable to sexually transmitted diseases (STDs) such as genital warts, gonorrhoea or herpes. Signs of STDs include blisters, warts or ulcers in the genital area, lower abdominal pain, and discharge from the vagina. The most common infection is chlamydia, which can lead to pelvic inflammatory disease, fertility problems and increased risk of ectopic pregnancy (in which the fertilised egg implants itself in the fallopian tube, rather than in the lining of the uterus). There is also an increased risk of cervical cancer. Warning signs which should not be ignored are: abnormal bleeding, pelvic pain, discharge from the vagina and pain when urinating.

Because of poor health in general, commercially sexually exploited women are likely to have more miscarriages and complicated pregnancies. Sometimes, women who become pregnant may feel that their only option is to have an abortion. In western countries, this is most often carried out by suitably qualified medical practitioners. When abortion is carried out by people without medical training and qualification, as it is in many settings throughout the world, it can lead to severe injury and even death.

Most women in prostitution have had at least one abortion. The use of contraceptives is so much a part of their working lives that they do not tend to use them in private relationships. If a woman is considering having an abortion, the key thing is to remain non-judgemental and discuss the options with her. Don't dictate what she should do. When Ellen, whom the team had got to know well, discovered she was pregnant, she became very upset. The problem was that this was her fourth pregnancy – the other three children had been removed from her by social services. When she asked Lydia for help, Lydia knew that she needed to be practical but gentle in her approach. She listened to her and showed her that she cared for her. She tried to help Ellen think through the realities and practicalities of her situation, and the options available to her. She didn't tell her what to do. When Ellen asked for an opinion, Lydia gave it, and gave the reasons why, but didn't pressurise her into conforming with her beliefs. Lydia hoped Ellen would decide against abortion, but resolved to stick by her even if she disagreed with her decision.

Commercially exploited women can be particularly vulnerable to HIV and AIDS. HIV (Human Immunodeficiency Virus) is responsible for AIDS (Acquired Auto Immune Deficiency Syndrome). HIV attacks cells known as lymphocytes, which are responsible for the body's immune system. This means that the body is more susceptible to infection and some types of cancer. The virus is spread by intimate contact of bodily fluids – blood, semen, saliva. It can be transmitted sexually, and by contact with blood or blood products – for example, in the use of contaminated needles used intravenously or in blood transfusions. It may also be passed from mother to child within the womb. Not everyone who becomes infected by HIV will develop AIDS, which is the final stage of infection. The progress of the HIV virus is unpredictable. Often the person has swollen glands and flu-like symptoms at the beginning, which then disappear. However, months later, many different problems can appear, such as infections, malignancies (cancers), neurological disease and muscle wasting.

There is no cure for HIV/AIDS. However, drugs have been developed which can relieve the symptoms and reduce the risk of infecting others. The earlier the infection is detected, the longer the person may be able to live with the disease. If there is any suspicion that a woman may be infected, encourage her to take an HIV test as soon as possible. If a woman seems ill or unable to shake off infections, don't be afraid to mention HIV testing – she will probably have thought of this herself and be relieved to have the issue brought out into the open. If possible, make sure that she is accompanied to hospital and clinic appointments. This will help offset the rejection that she may experience from other people.

Hepatitis B, C, and D are common infections and are associated with drug abuse. The hepatitis viruses cause severe infection of the liver. They are blood-borne infections which can be spread through unprotected sex or the sharing of needles. There is also a high risk of serious liver disease such as cirrhosis or cancer. Although not everyone who is infected goes on to contract liver disease, they may become carriers (that is, people who have the virus but do not have symptoms of the disease) and so might still infect others. The first symptoms of hepatitis are fever, tiredness, nausea, loss of appetite and general weakness. There may also be diarrhoea and vomiting. However, the main sign of hepatitis is jaundice (a yellow tinge in the skin and in the whites of the eyes), which may (but not always) appear one to two weeks after these symptoms have stopped and the person is feeling better.

Other problems can come from poor self-care, a chaotic lifestyle or neglect by others. There may be malnutrition, due to self-neglect or deprivation. Many women do not look after their oral hygiene; dental decay, whether it is due to neglect or high sugar use, has significant implications for a woman's overall health. Apart from the possibility of difficulty in eating certain foods, there is a risk of infection if bacteria from the mouth enter the bloodstream.

People who abuse alcohol are also vulnerable to diseases such as mouth, throat and breast cancer, stroke and heart disease, and liver disease. Drug users are very prone to infection generally; in particular, it is common for injection sites to become infected and abscesses may form. This could lead to gangrene and loss of the affected limb. Another risk is septicaemia (blood poisoning) which can be life-threatening. The risk of infection is greatly reduced if clean needles are always used for each individual dose. If there is a needle exchange service in your area, make sure the women know about this service and encourage them to use it. Drug abuse can mask pain, leading to conditions being left untreated.

We will discuss violence later, but in the meantime we can note that women are likely to suffer from broken bones, cuts, burns and head injuries inflicted by clients and pimps/perpetrators in vicious assaults and beatings. If you see signs such as bruising, cigarette burns, black eyes or grip marks, ask the woman how they came about, and where possible try to get medical help. A mixture of old and new bruises and wounds may suggest continuous abuse over a period of time. Often, though, if the perpetrator is the pimp, the woman may try to cover up the marks or attribute them to something other than abuse, for example an accident.

When people have suffered abuse and trauma for many years, the long-term health consequences can be severe. In a study undertaken on the health consequences of women who had been trafficked in Europe, many women were found to suffer from headaches, fatigue, dizzy spells, back pain, stomach/abdominal pain and memory problems.[50] Some health conditions may become chronic (that is, long-standing), and women can feel generally unwell, even long after they have stopped working in commercial sexual exploitation.

3. Damage limitation and health education

Most women involved in commercial sexual exploitation contract HIV through intravenous drug use and not through sex. They mostly practise "safe sex" by using condoms. Always advise women to use condoms and to have a supply with them as they work. Be aware, however, that while the women themselves may want to use condoms, they will have clients who are willing to pay extra for unprotected sex. Clinics can supply anti-allergenic condoms.

Using condoms helps to guard against STDs and hepatitis B, and reduces the risk of pregnancy. It is advisable, however, for women to use other forms of

---

50. *Stolen Smiles The Physical and Psychological Health Consequences of Women and Adolescents trafficked in Europe* London: London School of Hygiene and tropical Medicine 2006.

contraception too – for example, the contraceptive pill, implant, or intrauterine device. It may also be possible to get the emergency contraceptive pill.

Health education is an important part of your ministry. It can be done formally, as part the ministry's programme, and informally in every-day conversation. Many of the women will not know about safe sex and how to protect themselves – they are so focussed on making money, and so conditioned into thinking that they do not have any intrinsic worth, that they do not think about their health. One morning, on her way to work, Lydia decided to pop into the supermarket. She became aware that someone was calling her name. Edith, who hadn't been at the drop-in for a while, was standing at the entrance to the shop, propped up by a shopping trolley. Lydia had been praying that she would meet Edith, who was pregnant and still working. This, along with her drug addiction, made her very vulnerable indeed. (Her child would be very vulnerable too – pimps/perpetrators see the women's children as potential money-making machines, and sexually exploit them as they are growing up in exchange for accommodation, drugs and food. Thus, the generational cycle of commercial sexual exploitation is created). They chatted for a while, and Lydia took the opportunity to explain about the need to protect herself and her unborn child. Pregnant women were in high demand on the streets – men would pay triple the usual price. But the risk of injury to Edith and her unborn child from violent sex acts was high, and Lydia took the opportunity to explain this to her. Standing next to a freezer full of frozen pizzas she explained how vital Edith and her child were to Jesus and how much he loved her. She told her that there were some sexual services she must never perform for sex buyers because they could damage her and her baby (allowing them to put rods or bottles into her vagina, for example) and suggested some safer alternatives. She also explained the importance of having regular health checks, and that the team could help her to access them. Edith started to cry, overwhelmed that Lydia had taken the time to tell her these things. They prayed together, and when she got to

Health education can take place anywhere!

work, Lydia praised God for this encounter with a beautiful woman who matters so much to God.

4. Support in serious illness

If you are supporting a woman who has HIV/AIDS, hepatitis, cancer or any other serious and potentially terminal illness, make sure that you have your own support networks firmly in place. This will help you to keep spiritually and emotionally afloat. Learn as much as you can about the illness and how you can care for her, and do not work in isolation. We cannot give a comprehensive guide on how to care for someone with a serious illness but we can give some guidelines for ministry:

Try to help her to live in reality as much as possible, for only when she is able to see the situation in proper perspective will she be able to face up to her own mortality. She cannot do this if she is running away from reality in any way. If her life is chaotic and out of control, explain that this will exacerbate the illness.

Try to work through family problems with her. If contact with her family has been lost, and if reconciliation is possible and would be beneficial, try to help her to re-establish contact with them.

Encourage positive thinking. Has she any ambitions she would like to achieve e.g. taking an art course, sing in a choir? Her quality of life will be much better if she focuses on what she can do with the time left to her.

If possible, provide a community in which she feels welcome and safe. This may be church or a drop-in centre. Encourage her to become involved in support groups and attend specialist clinics if they are available in your setting.

Be sensitive to confidentiality. Discuss with the woman whom she would like to know of her illness and respect her wishes.

Stick with her. Remember the words of Christ: "I was sick and you looked after me." (Matt 25:36). Staying with someone who is ill and supporting them through treatment can be tough, but Jesus's words impress upon us that walking with people in pain and suffering is a central task for his followers. It can be an emotional roller coaster as diagnoses are given, new treatments tried, hopes raised, and disappointments encountered. Our role is a mixture of practical and pastoral help. Practically, you can help her attend clinic and hospital appointments, and make sure that she has everything she needs to be comfortable and safe. Pastorally, you can help by standing by her, and listening when and if she wants to talk.

Give concentrated support when she is first diagnosed and then back down slightly in order to prevent the development of an overdependent relationship.

If she gives you permission, pray with her. Discuss the illness with her, as well as the possibility of death. Try to help her not to react to the illness, and all that it entails, with bitterness, rebellion or unforgiveness, because these will only make her pain greater. Above all, keep assuring her of Christ's love for her, and pray that she will see that love through yourself and others.

5. Protection for outreach workers.

We have already suggested that it would be good for team members to have basic first aid training. If you employ staff, make sure that your health and safety policies adhere to legal requirements. Where possible, obtain medical advice as to the particular risks in your setting and what precautionary measures you should be taking – for example, vaccinations. In particular, you should have training in how to prevent infections, particularly those caused by contact with body fluids such as hepatitis and HIV. Here are some basic precautions which should be taken to protect staff and volunteers:

Have a clearly labelled sharps box in which to put contaminated needles and used razors. Find out from your local authority how sharps boxes should be disposed of. Keep the sharps box in a secure area.

Cover all cuts, however minor, with a waterproof plaster.

Wear disposable gloves when there is a chance of coming into contact with body fluids and discard them safely after use.

Ensure that clothes and bedlinen which are stained with blood, semen, vomit etc are washed immediately, using the washing machine's hot cycle.

If there is a major spillage of blood, burn the contaminated clothing if it is possible and safe to do so. Alternatively, place the clothes in two polythene bags labelled "CONTAMINATED CLOTHING" and arrange for disposal by your local authority. Always avoid touching the clothes with your bare hands.

If you suspect that a woman injects drugs, be careful if you have to handle her clothing – there may be hidden needles. Do not touch broken glass. Use paper towels, newspaper, card, or a plastic dustpan and put the fragments in the sharps container.

Burning blood stained clothes

It is advisable for outreach workers to be vaccinated against Hepatitis B. If any member of your team receives a needlestick injury, medical advice should be sought.

If eyes or mouth are exposed to blood or body fluids, wash copiously with water.

6. Cross cultural differences

An important part of our ministry, as we get to know the women better, can be to help them adopt healthier practices which will help them to live healthier lives. We can encourage healthy eating and good hygiene, for example, and help them to understand how these can help to improve their health generally. The needs will vary according to your setting. In western countries, for example, where obesity is an increasing problem, it will be helpful to talk about healthy eating, and even to help women learn basic cooking skills. In other settings, it may be important to help women learn about basic hygiene. Another important focus is prevention of illness and disease. For example, we can teach safe practices (such as using condoms and not sharing needles) which will help reduce the risk of HIV/AIDS. Find out what the pressing needs are, and try to make health education be as interesting, culturally appropriate – and fun – as possible.

Attitudes to health and ways of treating illness vary from culture to culture. If you are working in a culture different to your own, try to learn what the local attitudes and beliefs are with regard to health. There may be taboos and superstitions about certain kinds of health problems and their causes which seem strange to you. For example, in some Asian or African settings it may be that people believe that illnesses are caused by curses or magic. There may be different beliefs about childbirth and raising children with which you are not familiar, and there will certainly be differences of opinion about food and nutrition.

It is important to be sensitive to cultural differences such as these. Western Christians, for example, can unconsciously work on the assumption that western medicine is superior to other systems, and be shocked to find that not everyone shares this view. Although as Christians we would never go along with superstition, we should never assume that our way of doing things is superior – there may be a great deal to learn from local practices, and we should not dismiss local wisdom out of hand.

Lastly, remember that our physical well-being is related to our mental and spiritual health. As the story of the paralytic in Mark 2:1-12 shows (see below), the spiritual and social aspects of life are important for our health as well as physical wellbeing. The man was part of a community which cared for him enough to carry him and to break through the roof of someone's house! Then Jesus attended to the man's spiritual and psychological wellbeing by telling that his sins were forgiven. It is now well known that guilt and shame can have a detrimental effect on people's health and that forgiveness is central to our mental wellbeing. Our care of the women must therefore be holistic – we see them as whole persons and not simply as people to be healed or fixed. Social, psychological and spiritual care are as important for health as good nutrition and hygiene.

7. Following up…

Lydia admitted that she was disappointed when Ellen decided to have an abortion, but the team supported her in the days following the procedure. They knew they couldn't add another rejection to her life. Edith gave birth to a healthy boy, who was adopted by Edith's sister. As for Diane, she became so weak and tired that her pimp/perpetrator threw her out, saying she was no use to him. She was persuaded to see a doctor and was diagnosed with hepatitis. The team tried to persuade her to get treatment. At first, Diane was apathetic. She couldn't see the point in changing her lifestyle when she was going to die anyway. Eventually, though, she was persuaded that she could get better, and that this could be an opportunity to walk free from commercial sexual exploitation and addiction. She started the treatment, and went to a Christian residential drug rehabilitation centre where she gradually became stronger, and even agreed to go to a dentist! The team continues to support her. She now comes along to the drop-in and loves helping out, sharing her story with the women.

BIBLE STUDY

Mark 2:1:112

The healing of a paralysed man

Jesus has built up a reputation as a teacher and many people want to hear him speak. His authority is evident, and he is becoming famous. The friends bring the paralysed man to the place where Jesus is, going so far as to dismantle the roof to get their friend to him. To everyone's surprise Jesus deals first with his relationship with God and others, before healing his physical disability. Healing for Jesus seems to be holistic, rather than merely physical.

QUESTIONS FOR DISCUSSION:

> In Mark 2:1-12, why do you think Jesus focusses on forgiveness before healing the man's physical disability?
> What healthcare facilities are available in your area? Are they easily accessible? What health training would be most appropriate and useful for your team?
> Discuss your attitudes and beliefs about abortion. Are there differences of opinion in your team? How would you help someone who has had an abortion?
> Discuss how your team would go about supporting someone who has a chronic illness such as hepatitis B or HIV/AIDS.

CHAPTER 11

Mental Health Problems

"Praise be to the God and Father of our Lord Jesus Christ, the Father of compassion and the God of all comfort, who comforts us in all our troubles, so that we can comfort those in any trouble with the comfort we ourselves receive from God."

2 Corinthians 1:3-4

"Human beings are able to bear the unbearable only as others are willing to bear it with them"

Deborah van Deusen Hunsinger[51]

1. Introduction

AS THE DROP-IN became more established, an increasing number of women would visit in the evenings. They said they felt welcome there, and safe. For many, it was the first time they had ever felt valued and loved. Zoë (whom we met in the last chapter) became a regular. She was always bright and cheerful, no matter what was going on. She loved to crack jokes and laughed a lot. She especially loved having her long, beautiful hair braided by one of the volunteers. But gradually, Lydia observed a change in Zoë. She stopped joking and laughing and became irritable and bad-tempered. She seemed to jump at the slightest noise and began to accuse people of stealing her things. Lydia noticed that she had cuts on her arms, but Zoë refused to talk about what was troubling her and wouldn't let her contact the local mental health team.

The human mind is not able to cope with the abuse of the body which commercial sexual exploitation entails. Add to this broken family relationships and separation from children, and you can see that service users are highly likely to suffer from

---

51. Deborah van Deusen Hunsinger *Bearing the Unbearable: Trauma, Gospel and Pastoral Care* Grand Rapids: Eerdmans 2015, xiii.

mental health problems. The wounded mind cries out to be understood, and to be quiet and still. However, as long as the vicious cycle of exploitation continues, these cries of pain are drowned out by constant trauma and the wounds become deeper and deeper. Sometimes women have had a history of mental health problems before becoming involved in commercial sexual exploitation. Many women have come from backgrounds of neglect or abuse, and are likely to be prone to depression and mood swings, anxiety and possibly erratic behaviour. Chaotic lifestyles and a distorted sense of self which often results from selling sex are also contributing factors.

In this chapter, we will consider some of the mental health problems you are likely to come across as you reach out to service users. The most important thing you can do is listen, and as you do so it is helpful to be aware of some warning signs which might suggest that the woman is struggling and would benefit from being assessed by a medical doctor.

Unfortunately, in many cultural settings, mental health problems are viewed with great fear, and those who suffer from them are subject to ridicule, stigma and rejection which only serve to make matters worse. It is important that all team members have some understanding of the kind of difficulties women in sexual exploitation are likely to face, and to know the services which are available. Equally important is to be aware of your own preconceptions and reactions to mental health problems, and to understand the cultural views of mental health and ill health in the setting in which you are working. Taking all of this into account will help you to offer practical and sensitive support.

The most important thing is to listen

2. Stress, anxiety and fear

Zoë had managed to hide her symptoms for a long time, but gradually they began to take over. Of course, at first she buried her feelings and kept going for years in circumstances which most of us would find intolerable. However, it all became too much. She began to keep others at arms-length, trusting no one. And she became irritable, snapping at people, accusing them of things they hadn't done and driving them away. Clearly, no-one can live indefinitely with such a high level of stress, and for Zoë, self-harm became a way of coping with overwhelming feelings of anxiety and fear.

Because of the constant threat of violence, many women live in a perpetual state of anxiety and fear. Anxiety refers to a general feeling of unease, a vague feeling that something will go wrong. Anxiety can come about because of the general precarious nature of living – not having enough money, concern about accommodation, relationships with other people. Fear is more specific – for example, we might fear spiders or injury. Many women live in constant fear of assault from clients or their pimps/perpetrators or partners. It is normal and natural to experience anxiety and fear in situations like these, but these feelings can take over, becoming a constant presence. Women who are caught in commercial sexual exploitation live with such high levels of stress that they are always on the alert, looking out for danger. They can feel tense, irritable and restless. They may jump at sudden noises. Continuous stress can take its toll physically as well as psychologically. It affects sleep and appetite, and can cause poor concentration and irritability. It can be the cause of physical signs and symptoms such as skin rashes, headaches, arthritis, bowel disorders and heart disease. All this is the result of the continuous production of stress hormones which eventually damage the body.

3. Depression

Mental health problems can happen to anyone, regardless of culture or background, and severe prolonged stress is a major cause. When Nell (chapter 1) arrived in Chiang Mai she was bewildered by the change. The move from a tiny village to the huge city where she knew no one was difficult, but she was young and adaptable, and proud that she was able to send money back home to her family. However, the madam in the brothel where she worked made her work all the time, and she came to hate the work she was doing. All day long customers arrived – up to thirty a day – and Nell had to do whatever they wanted. She began to feel that she didn't exist anymore, that she had no future, and that her dream of learning to read and write would never be fulfilled. Nell began to feel that life wasn't worth living. By the time the outreach team came along Nell was severely depressed – withdrawn, almost silent, and thin from not eating.

The term depression is overused and misused. Many people say that they are feeling depressed when they are simply feeling a bit low or "fed up". True clinical depression, however, causes deep pain and suffering and can be life threatening. Some people become depressed because they suffer from bipolar illness in which there are extreme fluctuations of mood. Some are genetically prone to depression. Some women become depressed following childbirth (post-natal depression). Or there may be an organic cause such as a tumour in the brain. For some, there is no identifiable cause. However, depression can also develop as a result of severe life experiences. Women who have been involved in commercial sexual exploitation can become depressed, developing feelings of hopelessness and worthlessness.

Many women involved in commercial sexual exploitation live with depression. Some women disguise it by being busy all the time, or taking drugs or alcohol. Many more have symptoms of depression but soldier on, thinking that they are just part of life. In Nell's case, her circumstances had become so overwhelmingly difficult that she had developed a clinical depression and was hardly functioning. So how can we recognise this in someone? According to the DSM-5, if a person experiences five or more of the following, they may be said to be suffering from depression.

- low mood (a pervasive feeling of sadness)
- diminished interest in or pleasure in activities
- weight loss or weight gain
- inability to sleep or sleeping too much
- slowing down physically or feeling agitated
- excessive tiredness
- feelings of worthlessness or guilt
- poor concentration
- recurrent thoughts of death or suicide

So if, as we listen to a service user, it becomes evident that she has very low self-esteem, that she feels worthless and cannot see a future, we should begin to think in terms of depression. Is she complaining of vague aches and pains and of constant tiredness? Some people, like Nell, become very withdrawn and isolate themselves from others. They may be apathetic and their physical movements slowed down. Perhaps the most important signs are disturbed sleep patterns and a change in appetite. Some people find it difficult to get to sleep while others find that they waken at three or four in the morning and cannot get back to sleep. Some stop eating and lose weight, while others comfort-eat and gain weight.

The currently recognised treatment for depression is a combination of medication and counselling or psychotherapy. Of course, the availability of medical treatment for depression will depend on your setting. If treatment is available, you may be able to help by accompanying the person to appointments. In the main, however, your role is to offer pastoral support. Be there for her and be a listening ear. Reassure her of her inherent worth, and of her importance to God. So far as possible, make her feel welcome and part of a community. If she becomes isolated – try to keep in touch with her. Be patient, and be willing to forgive if she says hurtful things. Remember, however, that you cannot be there for her 24 hours a day, and that boundaries need to be established.

4. Self-harm

Many of the service-users we meet will engage in self-harming behaviour. This may range from taking overdoses of painkillers to burning themselves with cigarettes or cutting themselves with razors. Some take alcohol or drugs to numb the unpleasant feelings. This merely acts as a temporary anaesthetic, suppressing painful emotions for a while. Some women use self-harm as a coping mechanism. Skin cutting is the commonest method, using knives, broken glass or razor blades. Burning the skin, say with cigarettes or irons, is also common.

Self-harm can range from slight to severe – from superficial scratches to deep cuts. It used to be thought that people who self-harm were using it as a way to demand attention from others. As a result, they were often treated with disdain and lack of compassion. However, it is now understood that self-harm is a way of coping with internal pain. Much like drinking too much or taking drugs, self-harm helps the individual to relieve internal emotional pressure. However, self-harm provides only short-term relief and the deep pain does not go away. The best way to help someone who is self-harming is to provide an opportunity for them to express their emotions and concerns. The general advice is don't give up on the person, try to stay patient, don't reject her and don't give ultimatums ("unless you stop this I will….").

If someone comes to you who has cut themselves and you do not think the injury warrants medical attention, try to help them to dress their wounds themselves (this helps them to take personal responsibility for their actions). Be firm with them, but gentle at the same time. Realise that there are many underlying difficulties which are causing them to act in this way.

Repeated self-harm can be very difficult to deal with. It takes up a lot of time in casualty departments and emergency rooms and, understandably, clinicians can become impatient with and dismissive of those who self-harm.

5. Suicide

A woman who is feeling hopeless and depressed may indulge in increasingly reckless behaviour. For example, she may take serious risks such as going to sex buyers' homes, allowing her peers to exploit her, becoming embedded with violent abusers, or buying drugs from unknown dealers. She may speak of death and the desire to die and to end her life. If a service user speaks in this way, take her seriously and don't keep it to yourself. Discuss it with your team and encourage her to see a doctor.

Unfortunately, some service users will choose to end their own lives. This is always deeply distressing for teams, especially if you have got to know the woman and have become fond of her. Staff team and volunteers often feel that they should have done more and perhaps could have prevented the suicide. It is important to understand, however, that if a person has made up their mind to commit suicide, there is very little that one can do to prevent it. Ultimately, the responsibility lies with the individual herself.

If one of the women we are working with takes her own life, it is important that team members and volunteers are given a chance to talk about how they feel. For situations like this it is helpful to have someone who knows the team members and can act as chaplain. It can be very helpful to have a short liturgy in which prayers are said and people can remember her and honour her. Others who have been involved in her life can be invited to the short service – for example, family members and friends, workers from statutory bodies or other voluntary groups who worked with her.

Remembering and honouring

6. Trauma and PTSD

Women involved in commercial sexual exploitation are highly likely to have had adverse childhood experiences (ACE) of incest, child sexual exploitation and child abuse. Homelessness, and separation from families and children are normal for many, if not most, and as we have seen, they are constantly subject to violence, rape and enslavement. Each one of these might be described as "an inescapably stressful event that overwhelms people's existing coping mechanism",[52] but when you realise that the women may well have experienced some or all of them, and repeatedly over a long period of time, you begin to see how psychologically injured the women often are.[53] Judith Herman writes,

> "Traumatized people feel utterly abandoned, utterly alone, cast out of the human and divine systems of care and protection that sustain life. Thereafter, a sense of alienation, of disconnection, pervades every relationship, from the

---

52. Bessel A. Van der Kolk "Trauma and Memory" in van der Kolk et al *Traumatic Stress: The Effects of Overwhelming Experience on Mind, Body and Society* New York: Guilford Press 2007, 279.

53. See especially Melissa Farley (ed) *Prostitution, Trafficking and Traumatic Stress* Binghampton: Haworth Press 2003

most intimate familial bonds to the most abstract affiliations of community and religion. When trust is lost, traumatised people feel that they belong more to the dead than to the living." [54]

In repeated prolonged trauma, some people develop a coping mechanism known as dissociation, in which they are able to go through a traumatic experience and somehow remain psychologically detached from it. This is a coping mechanism which many women in commercial sexual exploitation develop. Unfortunately, according to Judith Herman, people who go into dissociative states are very likely to develop post-traumatic stress disorder.[55]

Many, if not most of the women with whom you come into contact will be suffering, to a greater or lesser extent, from post-traumatic stress disorder (PTSD). According to the psychiatric manual DSM 5, PTSD is characterised by persistently reexperiencing the traumatic event in unwanted memories, nightmares, or flashbacks. These vividly reproduce the original event, and cause the person to feel the emotions associated with it all over again. If an event occurs which reminds the person of the trauma (for example a loud bang might remind someone of an explosion in which they were injured), they may respond with emotional distress or a physical reaction. Someone who is going through this will try to avoid thoughts, places and situations which remind them of the trauma and the emotions associated with it. They may try to numb painful emotions by means of drugs or alcohol. They may become aggressive, hypervigilant, isolated and have feelings of anger, guilt and shame. If you suspect that someone is suffering from PTSD, if at all possible, encourage her to have specialised trauma counselling. If this is not possible, take time to listen, providing a safe environment in which she can begin to speak about the traumatic events.

7. Erratic, impulsive behaviour patterns

Many of the women with whom we work will find it very difficult to sustain regular hours, keep appointments, and maintain healthy relationships. Helping women to become less chaotic is part of the task of recovery, as we model reliability and stability. However, you will come across people whose behaviour seems particularly erratic, unpredictable and self-destructive. When Lola first came to the drop-in, she seemed to respond well in the friendly, non-threatening environment. Whenever she was feeling upset, she asked to see Lydia, who would spend a lot of time talking to her, encouraging her and helping her to calm down. Sometimes she would cut herself, and Lydia would help her to dress the wounds. Lola said that Lydia was the only person who had ever cared for her, and that because of her she

---

54. Judith Herman *Trauma and Recovery: The Aftermath of Violence -From Domestic Abuse to Political Terror* New York: Basic Books 2015 (1977), 52.
55. Herman *Trauma and Recovery,* 239.

wanted to leave commercial sexual exploitation. One day, however, Lydia was busy with someone else when she arrived at the drop-in and Lola became very angry. She turned against Lydia, said that she hated her, and that it would be her fault if she killed herself.

This kind of behaviour is a common pattern amongst women who are, or have been subject to repeated trauma, neglect, rejection and abuse, and is likely to be a coping mechanism which they have developed. A tendency to see people as only all good or all bad (known as "splitting") means that they may idolise someone who helps them when they first meet them, expecting them to fulfil all their needs and make them happy, quickly rejecting them when this does not prove to be the case. They tend to be deeply impulsive, restless, irritable, and subject to mood swings. They are prone to self-harm and making suicidal gestures. They can become very upset and tearful, or angry if they do not get what they want. They form very close, very intense relationships very quickly, but these just as quickly go sour, causing pain all round.

Naturally, all this is very difficult to deal with, and can take up a great deal of time, as they are very demanding of attention, constantly needing reassurance and encouragement. It is exhausting and frustrating, both for the person concerned and for those who are trying to care for her. It is important to understand that the behaviour is borne out of feelings of emptiness, boredom and lack of purpose. Above all, it stems from a deep fear of rejection and abandonment. Unfortunately, however, the pattern of behaviour only leads to repeated rejection and broken relationships, which increase her pain. Thankfully, most people who behave in this way calm down in their thirties. But before this happens much damage can be done and pain caused. It is true that women like Lola are extremely manipulative and demanding, but they are also very vulnerable. They do not realise quite how dangerous their volatility and impulsive behaviour is. They are likely to form intense sexual relationships with perpetrators, sex buyers and strangers, which put them into great danger.

The earlier you learn to detect this pattern of behaviour the better, for it is important to agree on strategies as to how to deal with it. The most important thing is to have firm boundaries. Ensure that meetings take place on neutral ground or in your project's premises. Don't be distressed or offended when someone who one day declares you to be her "best friend" on another turns against you and perhaps even makes false accusations against you. Where possible always have a witness with you – working in pairs for self-protection. Don't take things personally. It is crucial that we don't get sucked into the idea that we must constantly be available, or be deceived into thinking that we are the only ones who can help her. Understand that this kind of behaviour is itself in a sense a way of coping with the very deep trauma which most probably was part and parcel of her growing up. Don't respond with anger but with gentle firmness.

8. Following up….

Zoë's, Nell's and Lola's stories illustrate some very common mental health problems you are likely to meet. Eventually, Zoë began to talk. She had reached a crisis point and was afraid of everything, all the time, including the changes she knew she had to make. With the team's help she was able to leave her chaotic lifestyle, and for a while some medication from the doctor was needed to help her deal with the anxiety. Lola, unfortunately, disappeared shortly after her fall out with Lydia. It was rumoured that she had run away to another city and was working on the streets there, with a new pimp/perpetrator and a new name. Lydia felt sad, but with support she was able to reflect on what had happened and how best to deal with situations like this in the future. In Nell's case, the team helped her to leave the brothel. She was taken to a safe-house where she was loved and nurtured as part of the community there. Gradually she got her appetite back, gained in physical strength and began to see that there might be a future for her. She was able to learn how to read, train in a new skill and to continue to send money to her family. She never went back to the brothel again.

BIBLE STUDY

Read Mark 5: 1-20

The Story of the Gerasene Demoniac

In Palestine in the first century, it was generally believed that behaviour of the kind described in this story could be ascribed to demonic activity. Now, however we recognise that this man is seriously mentally disturbed – we would say that he is suffering from severe mental health problems. His behaviour resembles the kind of problems we might see among the women – tormenting thoughts, living among "tombs" such as addictions or destructive relationships or behaviour patterns, self-harm or self-destructive behaviour patterns, and an inability to have a stable life, or have healthy relationships. He has also been suffering for a long time and many attempts have been made to try to help him. Today, we deal with mental illness differently, understanding it to be caused by biological, psychological and social factors. But this story illustrates two abiding truths – dark powers constantly try take advantage of our human weakness and are bent on our destruction. Jesus, however, has complete power over them and can restore us to the people He wants us to be.

QUESTIONS FOR DISCUSSION

> Has anyone in your family been diagnosed with a mental health problem? If so, how do you feel about this?
> What mental health services are available in your setting? How accessible are they?
> How are mental health problems viewed in your cultural setting – are they feared? Ridiculed? Discuss how you can provide a safe place for women who are traumatised in your project.
> Have you ever worked with someone who behaves like Lola? What did you learn from the experience?
> What training do you think you and your team need to help you understand and deal with mental health problems?
> How can your project provide a community in which people who have, or are recovering from mental health problems can be safe?

CHAPTER 12

Addiction

At the core of every addiction is an emptiness based on abject fear

Gabor Maté

For I am convinced that neither death nor life, neither angels nor demons, neither the present nor the future, nor any powers, neither height nor depth, nor anything else in all creation, will be able to separate us from the love of God that is in Christ Jesus our Lord.

Romans 8:38-39

1. Jody

WHEN JODY (WHOM we first met in chapter 1) turned sixteen, Amir came into her life. Jody had lived in children's homes because her Mum couldn't look after her. She had always thought that no one would ever care for her, but Amir told her she was beautiful and gave her presents. Jody thought she had met the love of her life and dreamed of the day they would get married, but Amir was really "grooming" her for commercial sexual exploitation. After a while he gave her drugs and then made her have sex with his friends in order to pay for them. Jody soon slipped into a hopeless cycle of dependency. She found that she needed the drugs to help her to tolerate the old, fat men he made her have anal sex with, and the beatings he gave her when they complained that she didn't seem to enjoy herself. She needed the drugs even more when her baby was born and taken away from her – she needed the drugs to keep the pain of grief and shame away.

Many of the women we work with are affected, directly or indirectly, by drugs or alcohol. Drugs and alcohol are often readily obtainable and may even be supplied by pimps/perpetrators and madams. In this chapter we will look at how alcohol and drug addictions affect individual lives. We will also look at sex addiction and the fact that prostitution itself can become an addiction.

2. What is addiction?

Psychologist Mary McMurran describes addiction as follows:

> "A degree of involvement in a behaviour that can function both to produce pleasure and to provide relief from discomfort, to the point where the costs appear to outweigh the benefits"[56]

In other words, a substance is taken or an activity indulged in which gives short term pleasure or relief but which eventually results in severe difficulties, both for the individual concerned and those who care for them. Someone who is addicted to a substance or activity believes that they cannot live without it and continues to take it even when it is causing them serious harm.

There are differing views as to the nature of addiction. Many people think that addiction is a disease, whose symptoms and consequences can be treated. Others believe that there may be a genetic or inherited component. They argue that some people are born with a tendency to become addicted. A third view, which many psychologists hold, is that addiction is a learned behaviour which people take on to help them get through the pain of living, but which has got out of control. A variation of this view argues that addictions start out as behaviour which seeks to find relief in difficult circumstances and emotions, but that changes in the brain occur which mean that the behaviour becomes difficult to stop. However, the nature of addiction is very complex and, as is often the case, there is likely to be an element of truth in all of these theories. There can be little doubt that some families have more addiction in them than others. There can also be no doubt that some people seem to be able to control their drinking or drug taking. But many more find that the substance or activity becomes tyrannical in their lives, and when this happens ways of thinking and behaving develop which are so damaging and problematic to themselves and others that the person may aptly be described as having a disease.

At first, the pleasure and release which the drug induces is so rewarding that the person wants to experience it again and again. However, as use continues, increasing amounts are needed to make the world and life look tolerable again. Of course, all this demands more and more money. It also has a physical effect. At some stage, as the body becomes dependent on a regular intake of the substance, the person will begin drinking or fixing to relieve or avoid the symptoms of withdrawal, which can be profoundly unpleasant and debilitating. Jobs and relationships are lost, the person becomes increasingly isolated and health deteriorates, yet still the person persists. As Gabor Maté says, addicts "jeopardise their lives for the sake of making the moment liveable", even as their lives disintegrate:

---

56. Mary McMurran *The Psychology of Addiction* London: Taylor & Francis, 1994, 1.

"Nothing sways them from the habit – not illness, not the sacrifice of love and relationship, not the loss of all earthly good, not the crushing of their dignity, not the fear of dying. The drive is that relentless."[57]

Addicts learn to anticipate when withdrawal symptoms might step in and to time when to take the next dose to avoid any withdrawal whatsoever. For example, an alcoholic might leave enough in the bottle to relieve the symptoms of withdrawal which they know will occur in the morning. In Jody's case, Amir always made sure that drugs were available – so long as she worked to pay for them. Unfortunately, the more a person drinks or fixes to feel "normal", the less in touch with reality they are likely to become and the less able they are to take responsibility for themselves. Family, friends, health, employment all become secondary to the desire to drink or fix. Life gets out of control and the people they are closest to are hurt, with the addict himself or herself the last to realise or admit that those closest to them are suffering because of their actions, and that relationships have become strained to breaking point. It was because of her addiction that Jody's baby was taken away from her by social services – she just wasn't able to look after her.

3. Drug abuse

Where substances are concerned, there is a distinction to be made between misuse and dependence. Drug misuse refers to the use of illegal substances such as cannabis or ecstasy. It also refers to the use of prescription drugs – such as painkillers or sleeping tablets – for purposes not intended by your doctor. However, occasional use can become habitual.

Emotional Painkiller

Drug dependence comes about when someone finds that they cannot cut down or stop even if they want to. If a drug dependent individual stops taking the drug, they will experience physical symptoms of withdrawal.

People who are drug-dependent often (although not always) belong to a drug subculture; that is, they are part of a group of people whose lives revolve around drugs, who steal money to obtain them and become increasingly involved in crime. Life becomes increasingly chaotic and impoverished. Yet there can be a sense of

---

57. Gabor Maté *In the Realm of Hungry Ghosts: Close Encounters with Addiction* (rev ed) Toronto: Vintage Canada 2018, 28.

community amongst drug addicts. They share a common experience, know each other's needs (even if they cannot help meet these needs), and they get together to alleviate the loneliness of self-obsession. Addicts often score together (i.e. take drugs together) for company, for safety, or out of fear of overdosing.

Drug abuse is associated with many health problems. There is a high risk that the drugs available to the women you work with have been contaminated by other substances which make them cheaper to make, thus increasing profits for the criminals who produce them. Contaminated drugs can cause serious damage. As we write, in the United States and Canada there is a problem with fentanyl contaminated drugs, fentanyl being an opioid which is 40 times stronger than heroin and which causes overdose and death.

Health problems also arise from sharing needles. It is now well known that sharing dirty needles can be responsible for the spread of HIV and AIDS. Dirty needles can introduce other infections, such as septicaemia (blood poisoning), hepatitis, bacterial endocarditis (which affects the inner lining of the heart), and abscesses at injection sites. In order to minimise the risks, some health authorities provide needle exchanges from which clean syringes can be obtained in exchange for used ones. Prolonged intravenous drug use can also cause deep vein thrombosis (a blood clot in the vein which can prove fatal) or can lead to the veins becoming so punctured that they collapse. When this happens drug-users have to resort to ever more dangerous ways of injecting the drug such as using the veins in the groin.

Most drug addicts are unhealthy because of self-neglect. As the addiction takes hold, more and more money is needed to pay for the drug, and so less is spent on food. They will generally crave sweet things because drugs deplete a person's sugar levels. The need for instant gratification means that they are less able to have the patience to prepare healthy meals and attend to personal hygiene.

Drugs anaesthetise: they take away the ability to feel pain. This means that the person may not be aware of physical illness or see the need to go for treatment. Drugs also dull emotional pain. This means that people do not feel grief or disappointment, but it also means that they do not feel happiness and pleasure – other than that provided by the drug itself.

All this leads to problems at the point when people are able to stop taking drugs and go into recovery. When people stop taking drugs, they become aware of the pain caused, for example, by hepatitis, which can make the recovery process even more difficult and complex. However, it is even harder to face the build-up of trauma, regret, loss and hurt which addiction inevitably brings about. Years of anesthetising emotional pain means that people are unable to mature emotionally. Jody, who started using drugs at 16 and stopped at aged 26 dealt with hurt and stress in the same way as she did when she started, even though she was now ten years older. A major part of Jody's rehabilitation involved learning how to grow into emotional adulthood, which was hard and took a lot of courage. Jody was able to come through, but for many, this is partly what makes it so difficult and frightening even to contemplate change.

Drug addiction carries with it a host of other risks and dangers. The general public may be at risk from discarded injection equipment left in public places. Besides the obvious illegalities of drug dealing, a great deal of criminal behaviour is associated with addiction as people have to resort to criminal activity to fund their need for drugs. There is a great deal of violence amongst dealers as they mark their business territory and protect their profits. Lastly, there is great cost to tax payers as much police, medical workers' and lawyers' time is taken up with drug-associated crime. The cost to individuals, families and society is enormous.

Within street culture, the term "junkie" is often used to describe people like Jody. This has probably come about because of the use of the word "junk" for heroin, but the implication that Jody was also junk only added to her feeling of self-loathing. But Jody was not "junk". She was precious to God and her deep need was to have her self-respect restored and sense of self healed in Christ.

4. Alcoholism

The consumption of alcohol is legal in Western societies, however, in some Muslim countries, such as Afghanistan and Saudi Arabia, it is prohibited. In general, people drink for social reasons. Alcohol is used as a means of relaxation, to help people to talk and break down social barriers. However, alcohol must be used in moderation. As Proverbs 23 notes, when taken to excess, alcohol "bites like a snake, and poisons like a viper" (Proverbs 23:32). In other words, when drinking gets out of control, trouble starts. Alcoholism begins when a person starts to believe that she cannot function or relax without a drink. Eventually alcohol becomes the controlling factor in her life, often at the expense of family, marriage and employment.

As in all addictions, the main reason for abusing alcohol is to cope with or even avoid the difficulties of life. In severe alcoholism, the addict drinks to achieve a state of oblivion. The risks associated

Alcohol abuse

with alcoholism include physical, psychological and social damage. Physically, there is the risk of cirrhosis of the liver, oesophageal and liver cancer, stomach ulcers, malnutrition, stroke, heart disease, nerve and brain damage. Psychologically, memory and cognitive functions are affected. There may be selective memory in which the alcoholic remembers only the good parts of an event but fails to recall the bad behaviour which ruined the event for everyone else. This is called euphoric recall. Excessive drinking can cause blackouts, in which the person cannot remember events which took place during the binge. This kind of behaviour, in turn, leads to the breakdown of relationships as the alcoholic becomes preoccupied with drinking and less tolerant of those who object to their overbearing and selfish behaviour. Many crimes are committed by people who are under the influence of alcohol, and violence is common. As difficulties increase, the addict places herself outside of reality, building an impenetrable wall around her real emotions, unable to see that she is destroying herself.

5. Other forms of addiction

When the word addiction is mentioned, most people think in terms of drugs or alcohol. However, other things can cause addictions too. It is well accepted now that children who are allowed too much access to the internet can become addicted to video games. Some people are addicted to work – using it as a way to escape from unpleasant realities or thoughts. Even shopping can be an addiction – people can become hooked on the excitement of buying and the short-term pleasure of getting something new. Many men struggle with gambling because of the adrenaline rush that it brings. As we have seen, it is well known that many men who buy sex, also use pornography – which can itself become an addiction. Men and women who use pornography are seeking relief and comfort in just the same way as those who use alcohol or drugs, and the producers of pornography know this. However, those who use pornography (rather like those who use softer drugs but go on to use harder drugs) often want to act out what they see and read about – and this can bring severe suffering for women in commercial sexual exploitation. This adds to the perpetuation of violence within commercial sexual exploitation. Another problem is that using pornography desensitizes the user to the fact that the women they see in the films or magazines are human beings – they begin to see the models or actors as objects, without feelings or identity. This can contribute to the dehumanising of the women in prostitution.

Sex addiction also plays a large part amongst men who pay for sex. And as in other addictions, the behaviour is an attempt, consciously or unconsciously, to relieve emotional pain. Jay Stringer tells of man who attended a lecture of his in Seattle in which he suggested that our adult behaviour, including our unwanted sexual behaviour, is influenced by our family backgrounds. The man, who was single and had been arrested for soliciting women in prostitution, couldn't see the connection, saying that his parents were great people. It turned out, however, that this man's father had left his mother and that his life was now an endless round of taking his mother to doctor's appointments and church meetings. "I am glad I can love her so well," he said. "What I am trying to figure out, though, is why I always need to have a prostitute in my car after I get done spending time with my mom."[58]

This man was addicted to sex as a way of coping with the hurts and frustrations in his family life. In developing an addiction, he is no different to the millions of us who try to anaesthetise our pain in some way or other. The trouble is that as in other addictions there are consequences – and in sex addiction the consequences are self-loathing, self-contempt and shame, as well as the objectification of the people whose bodies are used.

6. Commercial sexual exploitation as addiction

One of the hardest things for Lydia and Tom to come to terms with as they gained experience in ministry was that involvement in commercial sexual exploitation can itself be an addiction. Gradually, they built up the contacts and skills they needed to help women leave their heart-breaking situations – away from abusive pimps and sex buyers, and into safety and freedom for the first time in their lives. Yet after a while some returned to the streets and brothels, back to the people who had controlled them and back to the violence and chaos. Lydia and Tom were deeply shocked and couldn't understand it. Why should this happen? Why would the women want to return to such suffering? Eventually they began to see that many women who work on the streets can become dependent not only on the income, but on the commercial sexual exploitation community itself. While there is ultimately very little loyalty, there is a camaraderie to be found there, and the women can find a sense of belonging and acceptance which they may not be able to find anywhere else. They may have built up relationships with pimps/perpetrators and sex buyers. And in the midst of all the trauma and suffering, they may even have found ways of making prostitution work to their advantage.

Tilly (whom we met in chapter 8), who had a history of repeated sexual trauma and abuse in childhood, found that she could use her pain to her advantage – when she finally broke free from the adults who had abused her, she learned to use skills that she had learned from an early age to earn money. Having grown up in an environment in which abusive sexuality was the norm, she found that continuing in this pattern could meet her own needs – for that was all she knew. Tilly sometimes found comfort in the physical closeness involved in the work itself and from the adrenaline buzz which accompanied the continual sense of danger and excitement. She could even use it to satisfy her own sexual needs, and, perhaps even more importantly, to

---

58. Stringer *Unwanted*, 18.

gain power over men who were dependent on her services. Having been hurt and humiliated all her life she could now hurt and humiliate men and earn money in the process. Although she had the opportunity to begin a lifestyle away from commercial sexual exploitation when Lydia took her to the residential rehabilitation centre, she found herself longing for the excitement of danger, and for the companionship and sense of identity it gave her, and for the sex buyers who sometimes flattered her and treated her like a princess. Although she knew her life was a kind of prison, leaving it entailed a loss which seemed too hard to bear. It took several stints in rehab before she was able, finally, to make the break and start a new life.

The fear of freedom

7. Treatment for addiction

Jody managed to get away from Amir, eventually. She turned up at the drop-in one night and heard, for the first time, that life didn't need to be like this, that she was loved by God and that she could get help to leave Amir and commercial sexual exploitation. After a few weeks, Jody asked God for courage to "step out of the boat" and leave. She agreed to go to a Christian drug rehabilitation unit, and so began a whole new way of life.

It was far from easy, though. Withdrawal from opiate addiction usually entails suffering severe flu-like symptoms and disturbed sleep for a few days. Withdrawal from stimulants such as methamphetamine and cocaine can lead to severe anxiety, agitation and disturbed sleep. People who are withdrawing from alcohol need medical supervision, for the abrupt stopping of very heavy drinking can be fatal. Medication can help get the person through the initial stages of withdrawal. For Jody, who had been taking opiates for a long time, the process was difficult, but even more difficult was the realisation that she had to learn new ways of thinking and ways of coping with the pain of everything that had happened to her. With the support of the staff at the residential drug rehabilitation centre, Jody thrived in her new environment, and was able to make a new start. She was also able to resist the pull to go back to her old life, to see just how destructive and harmful it had been, and began to build up a new, safe community and use her gifts and talents to help others.

BIBLE STUDY

Read Proverbs 23:29-35

Contrary to what many people think, the Bible does not say that people should not drink alcohol. As is well known, Jesus provided wine at the wedding in Cana (John 2:1-11). The Bible does, however, have a good deal to say about drinking to excess, acknowledging that too much alcohol can cause financial, emotional and moral ruin. Proverbs 23:29-35 contains a remarkably graphic and accurate description of the effects of an alcoholic binge and the subsequent withdrawal symptoms. Perhaps the best way to understand the Bible's approach is to see that what was intended for good and for our enjoyment has been perverted by the fall, and like many other things in life, can be misused. Although the question is not directly tackled in the Bible, we can be guided by the fact that in both the Old and New Testaments the teaching is clear that it is best for men and women to be in their right minds and sober (e.g. Ephesians 5:18)

QUESTIONS FOR DISCUSSION:

> How would you and your team go about caring for Jody?
> Have you any experience of addictions – personally or in your close family? What is the impact of addiction on families?
> Can the insights given about the nature of alcoholism in the Proverbs passage be applied to any forms of addiction other than alcoholism? If so, how?
> Why do you think so many people involved in commercial sexual exploitation are affected by substance abuse?
> In what ways does sex addiction and pornography use contribute to the continuation of the sex industry?

CHAPTER 13

Exiting, Recovery and Rehabilitation

No one can redeem the life of another, or give to God a ransom for them
Psalm 49:7

1. Introduction

ONE DAY, ALICE (chapter 9) announced she had had enough. She told Tom and Lydia that she wanted to leave Seb and get out of commercial sexual exploitation. She couldn't take the violence and pain anymore, and she wanted out. Tom and Lydia were delighted, but the obstacles seemed huge – what if Seb came after her? Where could she go that was safe? How could they help her come off drugs? What about her children? As Tom and Lydia thought about these questions, a new chapter in the life of their ministry began. Gradually, through trial and error, they learned how to enable people to walk away from commercial exploitation and live happy, dignified lives, free from fear and coercion.

2. Exiting

Many, if not most, service users express a desire to leave commercial sexual exploitation; however, only a few will actually do so. For most women, leaving prostitution is a momentous and frightening change. Of course, the implications of leaving will vary depending on the woman's circumstances. For those who have been trafficked across borders, exiting can mean 'escape' or disentanglement from immediate danger, long-term risk of retribution (against themselves or their families) from gang members, and new problems of reintegrating into their communities and finding other work. For women like Nell, who are under pressure to send money home, it can mean drastic change fraught with risks: how else are they to support their families or provide healthcare for elderly parents? For women who have no experience of any other life, it can mean leaving the only community and way of being they have ever known. So, while the desire to leave may be present, there

Should I go or should I stay?

are many barriers and obstacles to be overcome. Alice had thought a lot about leaving but the prospect was terrifying. How would she finance her drug habit? Where would she live? How could she get away from Seb, who was bound to come after her? Who would look after her? Seb might not be perfect, but at least he provided her with what she needed and she couldn't really envisage life without him. What would people say once they found out about her background? How would she get a job? Who would employ her? Commercial sexual exploitation was the only "work" she knew, and she had a criminal record.

You can see from all of this that leaving commercial sexual exploitation can be daunting and may even seem impossible. There are many complex difficulties to be overcome, and because of this it can take years of friendly encounters on outreach or in drop-in centres before someone is ready for transformational intervention. It is important for workers to realise the potential emotional and practical upheavals involved and to be sensitive, gentle and consistent in approach.

3. Steps towards recovery and transformation.

A report published in Britain has suggested that there are five stages in many women's move towards exiting – whether it be from street work or other forms of commercial sexual exploitation, including situations of sex trafficking. Whatever the story, whether they are working on or off the streets, the women are likely to have very similar experiences of violence, abuse and coercion, and have the same health needs. For example, those who work indoors are as likely to have addictions and suffer from severe trauma as those who work on the streets.[59] This is a useful guide which offers ways in which change may be facilitated – led by the women themselves. However, we are aware that it comes from a British context and you will

---

59. Julie Bindel, Laura Brown, Helen Easton, Roger Matthews, Lisa Reynolds *Breaking Down the Barriers: A Study of how Women Exit Prostitution* London: Eaves and South Bank University 2012. Https://i4.cmsfiles.com/eaves/2012/11/Breaking-down-the-barriers-a37d80.pdf (accessed 12/07/20)

have to adapt the material as appropriate for your setting, as the needs of women will vary. For Nell, who eventually realised that she may not survive if she stayed in the brothel, the priorities were learning to read and gaining a new skill. Thankfully, she was able to enter a specialised centre run by Christians which taught her new skills and gave her employment. Alice, as we shall see, had different hurdles to face. As in all such paradigms, there is no one size fits all and some women will progress quickly while others will take years with many lapses and setbacks.

3.1. Stage one. Readiness and engagement.

In this initial stage, women begin to express the desire for change in their lives. Alice expressed the desire to quit but was unsure about how or when this could happen. She knew she needed to leave, because life was becoming intolerable. There had been a gradual change in her perception of her life before she spoke to Tom and Lydia. She was tired of the violence and wanted to get away from Seb. She began to speak more about the overwhelming emotional distress she was suffering and of how ill she felt. After a while, she concluded that, despite the great risks involved, the advantages of leaving outweighed the disadvantages.

3.2. Stage two. Treatment and support.

At this stage, women become more willing to accept help and become more actively engaged in bringing about change. Alice began to connect more with the team and the agencies which could help her – for example, rehab units, counsellors and social workers. This was an important move forward, for it was more than just expressing a desire – it was a conscious effort on her part. The team helped her to identify her needs and to access the agencies which could help. Alice agreed to go to a Christian residential drug rehabilitation centre and completed the programme there.

3.3. Stage three. Transition and stabilisation.

This is a period of transition in which various issues are addressed. Alice began to tackle very personal things– relationships with family, friends and psychological issues. This took a lot of time, and patient listening on the team's part as they tried to help her to make sense of her experience. Where possible, discussions took place with specialist agencies and support groups. Alice had gone through profound trauma, and needed help to process this and recover from the trauma of commercial sexual exploitation. As Judith Herman notes,

> "The core experiences of psychological trauma are disempowerment and disconnection from others. Recovery therefore is based upon empowerment

of the survivor and the creation of new connections. Recovery can take place only within the context of relationships; it cannot occur in isolation."[60]

Alice started to receive counselling from a specialist psychotherapist. The team helped her through this painful process and at the same time enabled her to tackle practicalities such as housing and finance. After rehab, she needed to find a safe place away from Seb and from her friends on the streets who had been encouraging her to stay there, and access to money for basics.

3.4. Stage Four. Reconstructing and Rebuilding

At this stage, life becomes less chaotic and more stable. The past begins to be addressed, and a new future prepared for. The team was delighted when Alice managed to get an apartment well away from the area she had lived in with Seb, and away from the streets she had worked in. She was honest enough to say that she missed some of her old friends, but realised that if she got in touch with them, she could easily fall back into old patterns. Alice kept in touch with people she had met in rehab, and began to attend church, where she made new friends. She often talked about seeing her children but realised that this might not be possible.

3.5. Stage Five. New Roles and Identities

At this stage, women make determined efforts to develop a new life and identity, Alice started to gain new skills so that she could get a job. She volunteered in a social enterprise café which helped train people for employment. She continued with counselling, and worked with a tutor to help improve her literacy and numeracy skills. She began to talk about the future in a hopeful, positive way. She continued with counselling, which helped her to develop new ways of coping when life became stressful. She was no longer controlled by coercive relationships or damaging peer groups, but is learning to think for herself and make healthy choices.

4. Tips for teams

The best advice we can give here is – try to avoid the temptation to drive change yourself. This can be very destructive, even if done from the best of motives. Women need to recognise their own need for change, rather than be told by others. Our desire to see transformation is not the issue here, and if this is the driving force in the relationship it can take years before a genuine request for help comes voluntarily from the woman.

We can, however, open the discussion about exit as a realistic and achievable option. It can be helpful to run sessions about exiting entitled "I want to leave" in which we outline the possibilities and the help available. We can play a major

---

60. Judith Herman "Recovery from Psychological Trauma" <u>Psychiatry and Clinical Neurosciences</u> 52 (2002), 98-103.

role by listening and helping the woman to make up her own mind. It is not your job to persuade her to leave. It is your job to help her weigh up the pros and cons of exiting – if she expresses the desire to do so – and to help her to understand her motivations for change. Be prepared for a long haul and do not expect that change will come quickly. Over thirty years of experience has taught us that it takes, on average, between 5 and 7 attempts for women who work on-street to exit commercial sexual exploitation.

Don't try to drive change

Exit can only be facilitated, not forced. As we have seen, women need to be enabled to articulate their own change of thinking, and this can be a long process. They need to be listened to and helped to think through consequences, rather than told what they should be doing. You cannot force anyone to want to leave – you cannot tell them to do so, you cannot even persuade. The desire for change can only come from her – our job is to have faith and let God work in their lives.

Don't make things too comfortable. Serving the women can facilitate change but it can also disempower. It is possible to be so welcoming and so focussed on conveying unconditional love that we fail to create transformational possibilities. For example, the drop-in can simply be too cosy, or provide so much that women are (unintentionally) enabled to continue in destructive lifestyles. Tom and Lydia discovered this one night when Tilly said, "Thanks so much, you've helped me to face another night out there." They realised they were running the risk of helping Tilly to continue as she was rather than enabling her to think about change. Not only that, we were indirectly enabling Frank, her pimp/perpetrator, to continue exploiting her. When outreach and drop-in services don't inspire or facilitate recovery, an exploited woman ceases to journey into freedom and becomes a user of services. Christians, remembering Jesus' demand that we feed, clothe and care for people who are ill, and visit those who are in prison – "the least of these" (Matthew 25:40) can fall into a trap of doing this to such an extent that we disempower those whom we are trying to help, making people dependent on us, hindering them from learning how to care for themselves. Part of caring is helping people to develop and grow into independence. We can infantilise and stultify, which is not what Jesus intends.

Unconditional love does not mean unconditional acceptance of behaviour. Knowing how to convey unconditional love while keeping boundaries and safety for all requires constant assessment and prayer by the team as a whole.

The problems listed above do not go away overnight, and women will need patient help to find work, housing and deal with outstanding debts and so forth. Many women will have children, and there may be painful times as they face the reality of not seeing or being separated from them. Other painful times may have to do with trying to mend broken relationships with families and children, and learning to live with the consequences of past actions which have caused hurt not only to the woman herself but to those who were closest to her.

Recovery from multiple traumas takes a lifetime of compassionate accompaniment and listening. When women have been living in chaotic lifestyles it can take a long time to learn how to live quietly and without the dramas to which they have become so accustomed. Expect progress to be slow. Celebrate small victories and be patient if it seems to be a case of one step forward, two steps back.

The past still had its effect on Alice's life – there were broken relationships, ill health, and feelings of remorse, shame and guilt to deal with. She needed help to get back in touch with her family, and to face realities such as whether she could or could not get her children back. In Alice's case, this was not possible – they had been taken into care because of the toxic environment they had been living in. It also had to be acknowledged that Seb was likely to be out to harm her, and ultimately, to destroy her.

In general, men tend to see recovery in terms of task, of a programme to follow. Women, however, tend to see recovery in terms of relationships. If they have children, this will be a major concern. This adds a further layer of complexity in the women's lives. Many, like Alice, have had children removed from them and put into foster care or adoption. This is usually because of drug or alcohol abuse which means that they are unable to look after their children. Some will persist in some unhealthy sexual relationships as this is what they know. Many others will decide that they want nothing whatsoever to do with men.

If you have a centre or drop-in, try to have a separate entrance and area for women who are in recovery. In this area you can focus on areas for development – such as personal responsibility, learning to keep appointments, how to be part of a healthier community, writing CVs and applying for work, developing new coping mechanisms and having fun in new ways.

If you are in a setting where social services are present, liaise with them to ensure "joined up" care and support. For example, in some areas, local councils will be quick to give a woman a flat if she is escaping violence. However, without adequate support, and if this is done too early before she has learned to make better choices, she might easily revert to the ways she knows, her home becoming a brothel or crack house.

If you are working with women who have been trafficked from outside the country, work with a trusted translator where appropriate. This is especially important for health, legal and administrative appointments. Lack of understanding can greatly add to the suffering and increase the risk of imprisonment, deportation and detention.

Be aware that someone who manages to leave commercial sexual exploitation may experience a profound sense of loss. She will have left behind a sense of identity, belonging, and relationships. The realisation of the damage that has been inflicted upon her by violence and addiction can be unbearable and too painful to face in order for healing to start. Don't be surprised if she leaves one addiction and replaces it with another.

Some women will return to commercial sexual exploitation, even after some time of freedom and learning new skills. You will find this difficult, and even incomprehensible. Remember, however, that for many women prostitution is an addiction, and that the familiar can seem deeply comforting, even if it is destructive and harmful.

5. Rehabilitation

Since Alice was trapped in drug addiction, detox and treatment were vital, as was finding the right method of rehabilitation. The same goes for people with alcohol addiction. For some, counselling and support will be sufficient but for Alice, and indeed most others, a Christian residential rehabilitation unit was the best option. This had many advantages. It took Alice out of the toxic environment which had been doing so much harm, nursed her through physical withdrawal, and gave her the time and space to develop new relationships, healthy habits, and a new philosophy of living. Alice had been escaping from life for many years; she needed to learn how to be honest with herself and begin to take responsibility for her actions. She needed to be able to learn to cope with the crippling sense of shame which could so easily lead to relapse. In other words, she needed to learn how to forgive herself and others.

If a woman asks to go to a residential drug rehabilitation centre, try to help her articulate her expectations and motivation. It may be that what she really wants is to keep away from certain people on the streets, or to avoid a custodial sentence. If this is the case, successful completion of the programme is less likely, but not impossible. Usually a deep desire for change is necessary. Be realistic about what residential rehabilitation can do and tell her what she might expect. Discuss the options with her, and if she persists in wanting to do this, make every effort to help her. If possible, try to find a rehab centre away from the drug environment – away from peer group pressure, and from which it will take some effort and determination to leave. Where possible, too, try to find residential rehabilitation centres staffed by people who understand the particular needs of sexually exploited women, and can provide specialist counselling. It is helpful for the woman to have as much written information about the centre as possible before she goes – about its routines and philosophy, as well as practical things like room-sharing and bathroom facilities.

The application process can be lengthy and frustrating, depending on your setting. If the centre is not dependent on government funding, things tend to be more straightforward. Where relevant and appropriate, make sure that you keep lines of communication open and liaise with statutory bodies such as social workers, doctors, probation officers and so forth, keeping the woman informed at every step of the way.

Be understanding. Going to a rehab is a huge step to take. Change tends to be frightening for most people, but for an addict the prospect of facing life's hurts without emotional painkillers can prove too much. If she does decide to go, be supportive during her stay, visiting and contacting, sending cards and praying for her. She may be asked to sign a contract which means she is not allowed visitors or to leave the unit unaccompanied in the first weeks. It is helpful to know the rules of the house so that you can support her in sticking to the terms to which she has agreed.

Going to Rehab

Everyone finds rehab difficult. Not only do they have to discover how to be drug free, they have to learn to face the future without drugs or alcohol, change thinking habits and plan for a new life without previous friends and accomplices. Some will not be able to tolerate the programme and will not last the course. Some people have been to many centres and through several programmes and still struggle. This is par for the course, and it is important that you do not become overwhelmed by disappointment.

Continue to be supportive after the woman leaves the rehab centre. A safe community in which people are valued and enabled to grow is essential.

But be careful to create a culture of empowerment rather than dependency and passivity. Long-term transformation of women's lives means focussing more on recovery and less on crisis intervention and aid. In other words, we are committing to lasting relationships, journeying with the women as they prepare for and go through change and persevering with them in hope.

6. Moving forward

From the way we have told Alice's story here, you might think that the transformation in her life was relatively easy. It wasn't. The consequences of a time in sexual exploitation are never obliterated. She had to be supported to face the emotional upheaval and practical difficulties that she experienced in the process of exiting. Today, she continues to have a mentor who helps her sustain her new way of life, who encourages her and helps her to make wise choices. And just like everyone else, she needs to be part of a healthy community which prizes her, weeps with her in the hard times and rejoices with her in the good (Rom 12:15). As for Tom and Lydia, they had a lot to learn as they helped Alice to exit commercial sexual exploitation. They had to liaise with other organisations, work with people who had expertise in certain areas, and be gentle but tenacious. Above all they had to keep praying, looking to God for the gifts and wisdom that they needed as they helped Alice find new life and walk into freedom.

BIBLE STUDY

EXODUS 14:21-22

"Then Moses stretched out his hand over the sea, and all that night the Lord drove the sea with a strong east wind and turned it to dry land. The waters were divided, and the Israelites went through the sea on dry ground." (14:21-22)

It is important to read the whole of chapter 14 in order to place these verses in context. The people of Israel have fled Egypt, and Pharaoh is pursuing them. The slaves were trapped, perhaps hopeless and gripped with fear, yet God gave them freedom of choice to engage in recovery. At first, they "march out boldly" but when they saw the Egyptians catching up on them, they started complaining to Moses, thinking that they are going to die. It looks like they had thought things would be straightforward but they have turned out to be more complex and difficult. Moses tells them to stand firm. God tells Moses to move the people forward, provides the protection and guidance of an angel and a pillar of cloud, and enables the people to break free from the Egyptians. It is interesting that when the people of Israel eventually do reach freedom, they are recorded as longing to return to Egypt, where food was available. They found the freedom difficult to cope with.

QUESTIONS FOR DISCUSSION

> What services do you, or would you like to, provide in your ministry? How can you avoid enabling people to continue in destructive lifestyles and patterns?
> What insights does the story in Exodus 14 give us about human nature?
> Discuss how your team might go about helping Alice to leave her life of commercial sexual exploitation.
> Exiting is an unknown experience compared to the familiarity of slavery in Egypt. It can seem terrifying and even impossible, and can be more difficult than we might expect. From your reading of Exodus 14, how does God enable his people to escape their life of slavery?
> Do the steps for exiting and recovery which we have outlined here ring true for your cultural setting? If not, why not, and how can you adapt them for your ministry?
> What practical issues are likely to crop up in your setting as you help women exit commercial sexual exploitation?

CHAPTER 14

Discipleship

"All authority in heaven and on earth has been given to me. Therefore go and make disciples of all nations, baptizing them in the name of the Father and of the Son and of the Holy Spirit, 20 and teaching them to obey everything I have commanded you. And surely I am with you always, to the very end of the age."

Matthew 28:18-20

1. Introduction

ONE DAY, LISA accidentally stumbled across a Christian drop-in centre. There, she was introduced to the Bible, and in three days, she had read the whole Message New Testament and had learnt Psalm 27 by heart. Soon, with the help of the team, she had a plan to leave commercial sexual exploitation and to start a new life. She is now employed as a youth pastor, and draws on her experiences in her work. She also spends time with other victims of commercial sexual exploitation, listening to them with compassion and selflessness, and sharing her unique wisdom with them. Her experience of suffering and redemption are being used to comfort others (2 Cor 1:3-4). Lisa is able to relate to these women and girls in a way that others cannot. They trust her and know that she understands.

Lisa's progress was nothing short of miraculous and she continues to be an inspiration to us all. But she, like all other Christians, needed help to persevere in her new found faith and to grow and mature – in other words, she needed to be discipled. In this chapter, we will give some pointers for discipling people who are or have been caught up in commercial sexual exploitation. The word "disciple" means "learner" or "apprentice", so when we become followers, we become students or apprentices of Jesus himself. We begin to absorb his teachings and to be in relationship with him.

2. Understanding Discipleship

What is the difference between recovery and discipleship? A person who is in recovery is learning strategies for coping. A person who enters into discipleship, on the other hand, starts on a lifelong adventure of relationship with Christ, and of learning how to live in a way that is pleasing to him. Romans 6 speaks of being a new creation after baptism, and John's gospel speaks of believers being reborn (John 3:3). But this does not mean that we become perfect after conversion, or that there should be no more trouble in our lives. Rather, it means that we begin afresh and that we enter into a new journey of learning how to grow into maturity, and becoming more like him. Part of this means finding our place in the church, and how we can best serve others.

Discipleship is a lifelong journey. It is our job, as people already on that journey, to be partners to those who join us on the road, sharing what we have learned. We are guides because we have gained some experience. But we are not their superior, for we are still students ourselves. We are simply a little further down the road. We are all teachers and we are all learners. We, too, have come from darkness into the light, and are learning what that means. Nevertheless, those who have come from backgrounds of commercial sexual exploitation do need special understanding and spiritual sensitivity. Their lives have been eaten away by locusts (Joel 2:25), and it is our privilege to accompany them as God restores these years to them.

A little further along the road

3. A Twelve Step Model

Many Christian residential rehabilitation centres use versions of Alcoholics Anonymous' Twelve Step programmes help people become free of addiction, but the model can also be used for discipleship. The premise is that we <u>all</u> start out from brokenness, addiction and powerlessness. We <u>all</u> need to rely on God completely to help us to learn to walk in the freedom of Christ. Twelve Step programmes help us to exchange our destructive tendencies and choices for good, healthy ones, and

Discipleship

to learn to let go of what is keeping us from the freedom of surrendering to him. In his book *Breathing Under Water*, Richard Rohr explains how this pattern can be applied to spiritual growth, and we will draw on this here.

Step 1: We admitted we are powerless over our addictions, that our lives had become unmanageable. According to Rohr, this is the hardest step to take,

> for most of us do not want to admit that we are powerless. We like to think that we can sort ourselves out. However, the paradox is that we are at our strongest when we are at our weakest (2 Corinthians 12: 9-10): admitting our weakness gives God the space to step in: "Unless a kernel of wheat falls to the ground and dies, it remains only a single seed. But if it dies, it produces many seeds" (John 12:24)

Step 2. We came to believe that a power greater than ourselves could restore us to sanity. We begin to lean on God, learning to understand the gift and healing of worship. It is the beginning of hope: "The eternal God is your refuge, and underneath are the everlasting arms. He will drive out your enemies before you" (Deuteronomy 33:27). Many of us struggle at this stage, delaying the decision to surrender ourselves to God, as we resist losing control of our lives.

Step 3. We made a decision to turn our will and our lives over to the care of God as we understand him. At last we make the decision to surrender our wills to him. Our own way of running our lives hasn't worked, and we must trust in His infinite goodness: "Ask, and it will be given to you; seek and you will find; knock, and the door will be opened to you". (Matthew 7:7).

Step 4. We made a searching and fearless moral inventory of ourselves. This is about being honest with ourselves, no longer running away from the fact that, in our arrogance, we have hurt ourselves and other people. We admit our faults, flaws and limitations, realising that when we do so grace can be "even greater" (Rom 5:20-21 NLT). Only with such self- awareness, Rohr says, and exposing our darkness to the light, will our behaviour be transformed.

Step 5. We admitted to God, to ourselves and to another human being the exact nature of our wrongs. Christians have always recognised the value of confession (James 5:16). Acknowledging our sin and failure to a trusted mentor is the basis for healing and forgiveness. Confession is a humanizing encounter that liberates and is a direct encounter with God's love. We are "real" about ourselves and so the way is paved for relating to others with integrity and honesty.

Step 6. We were entirely ready to have God remove all of these defects of character. At this stage we begin the hard work of "getting out of the way" and letting God work in our lives, rather than relying on what we ourselves think we can do. We begin to realise that the "It does not, therefore, depend on human desire or effort, but on God's mercy" (Romans 9:16).[61]

---

61. Rohr's paraphrase.

Step 7. We humbly asked God to remove our shortcomings. Prayer is the bedrock of spiritual growth. Its purpose is not to get God to do things for us but to be in a relationship with him. We are completely dependent on him for we cannot transform ourselves: "Have mercy on me, O God, according to your unfailing love; according to your great compassion blot out my transgressions. Wash away all my iniquity, and cleanse me from my sin." (Psalm 51:1-2)

Step 8. We made a list of all persons we had harmed and became willing to make amends to them all. It is imperative that we go back and try to repair what we have broken. If we are to blame for damaged relationships, then we can try to mend them by admitting our mistakes and apologising for hurts caused. Those we have hurt may not always want to embrace us, but the willingness to make the attempt signifies a desire to bring healing and shalom (peace) into God's world: "if you are offering your gift at the altar and there remember that your brother or sister has something against you, leave your gift there in front of the altar. First go and be reconciled to them; then come and offer your gift (Matthew 5:23-24).

Step 9. **We made direct amends to such people wherever possible, except when to do so would injure them or others.** We have to take active steps to have open and honest relationships, but this needs to be done wisely. There are times when broaching certain subjects might open up old wounds, making things worse. Our own spiritual need for honesty and confession should not be at the expense of others. "If any of you lacks wisdom, you should ask God, who gives generously to all without finding fault, and it will be given to you" (James 1:5).

The Twelve Steps

Step 10. We continued to take personal inventory and when we were wrong promptly admitted it. Jesus asks Peter three times if he loves him (John 21:17): this relationship is a work in progress. Are we continually open to God, or are we falling into old habits of attachment to other things? It is easy to fall into spiritual arrogance or complacency and to think that we have finally "made it". We haven't! We need to be open and realistic about our capacity for failure – not to beat ourselves up, but to acknowledge with gratitude that grace lifts us up over and over again.

Step 11. We sought through prayer and meditation to improve our conscious contact with God as we understood him, praying only for knowledge of His will for us and the power to carry that out. In other words, we make "conscious contact with God" the mainstay of our lives. As we do this, our lives become wholly oriented towards God and His will rather than the fulfilment of our wishes and desires. As our hearts are changed, we find ourselves looking at the world through His lens rather than our own. As Rohr says, "Prayer is not about changing God, but about God changing us."[62] Praying and meditating in quiet surrender heals the soul: "the kingdom of God is within you." (Luke 17:21 ASV)

Step 12. Having had a spiritual awakening as a result of these steps, we tried to carry this message to others, and to practise these principles in all our affairs. Jesus said to Simon Peter, "Simon, Simon you must be sifted like wheat, and once you have recovered, you in your turn must strengthen your brothers" (Luke 22: 31).[63] Our spiritual development, with all its struggle and blessing, is not for our own good only; we must use our experience and gifts to reach out to and help others to grow in faith. Grace is so precious a gift that we must share it with others. Our encounter with the love of God will result in love for others.

No two people's journeys are the same, and we all grow at different paces. There will be periods of obvious growth, and periods when it looks as if nothing is happening at all – that we are standing still. There will also be relapses and mistakes. The habits and attitudes which are the result of commercial sexual exploitation can take years to unlearn. But the story of God's dealings with his children is one of constant grace – we stumble and we fall, and He graciously helps us back on our feet and enables us to learn from the mistakes that we have made. As disciples, we need to ask him to enable us to be gracious and wise as we accompany others.

In Lisa's case, on the surface, the journey was relatively smooth. She had been introduced to the gospel through a student outreach, seen the possibility of a new way of life, and left commercial sexual exploitation. She had run away from home at 16 because her uncle had abused her. No one in her family had listened to her, so when she met the students and went to their church, she felt a sense of belonging she had never had before. Lisa presented well, and her middle-class accent meant that she fitted in very quickly. She was also clever, and soon learned what to do and say to be accepted. No one would have thought that she had a past in commercial sexual exploitation.

---

62. Rohr *Breathing under Water* Kindle location 96.
63. Rohr's paraphrase

But Lisa's strength was also her weakness. It was easy for her to gain the externals without inner transformation. It was as if she started her journey at stage six – without the hard work of confession and repentance. But "heart work" must come first if our faith is to be more than external conformity to social and cultural norms. Thankfully, Lisa came to see that something was missing, and with the help of a faithful and gentle mentor, she was able to work through her trauma and grow into the person whom God could use to be a mentor and guide to others.

4. Hints for disciplers

Ideally, discipling should be done through the church. But if this is not possible, have a designated person to take on that role. Keep the tasks and roles distinct: for example, other team members can take care of practical issues. Meet the person regularly and pray with her. Help her to find a church – one in which she feels welcome and whose worship style she enjoys. Alpha courses are good introductions to Christian teaching.

Unfortunately, not all churches are hospitable places for people who are involved in commercial sexual exploitation. There are still some communities (like Pastor Joe's in chapter 3) which shun rather than welcome those who have been involved in prostitution. If you are unable to find a welcoming community, you may have to provide it yourselves.

Don't insist that women who become Christians leave commercial sexual exploitation. A desire to leave should be a natural outcome of becoming a follower of Jesus and not a condition. Jesus did not demand that people had to change their lifestyle if they were going to spend time with him, as his reputation for being a glutton and drunkard shows (Luke 7:34). He wanted them to see who He was, and change followed on from that. There is a practical reason for this, too. In some areas of the world, prostitution may be the only way that the women can earn a living or be able to support their families. So, if we want them to come out of commercial sexual exploitation, we will have to be able to offer realistic opportunities and alternatives.

If there is a chemical addiction, encourage the person to go into a Christian drug rehabilitation centre, and support her in her application.

Meet regularly for prayer and Bible Study. Find Bible study tools which are culturally appropriate and easy to use. Reading through the gospels in groups or with individuals helps people to focus on Jesus' own teaching. Reading Paul's epistles is useful for helping them think through what it means to live in community. Victims of commercial sexual exploitation often lose an understanding of what it means to have good, trusting relationships. They are used to people using them, and are accustomed to betrayal and abandonment. One of the first things to teach is trust and what this means in everyday relationships with other believers. As part of this, it is good to help people learn basic Christian ethics – the ten commandments are a good place to start. However, it is vital that you encourage discussion as to <u>why</u> these commandments are there in the first place – <u>why</u> it is important not to steal or to lie, for example. Some new believers struggle with this – "I'm an individual, why can't I do what I like? You tell me that Jesus has set me free, but why are there so many rules?" Like the people of Israel when they left the slavery of Egypt, those who come out of slavery today need help to understand the nature of freedom. Moses brought the commandments from God, precisely to enable God's people to build up trusting relationships with God and others – not simply to stop us enjoying themselves!

An Alpha Course programme can help give Biblical insights. It can also be life-changing, as Suzanne found out during the teaching on the Holy Spirit. She was instantly freed of pain after months of sleepless nights and suffering.

Experiment with different ways to explore the Bible. Storytelling crosses cultural boundaries and you can have a lot of fun trying out different ways of telling Biblical stories – using video, drama, or role play. Women often respond well when pictures and everyday objects are used to help them to make links between the Biblical stories and their own experience. Another useful tool is Contextual Bible study.[64] This is a method of reading the Bible in groups which encourages participants to relate what they are reading to their personal experience and context. The emphasis is not so much on the leader explaining what the passage means, as on enabling people to discover what it might mean themselves.

It is helpful to introduce New Testament teaching on sex and sexual relationships. Women who are used to promiscuity often come to believe that their bodies are somehow detached from themselves – that sexual relationships have no effect at all on their psyche or spirit. The teaching of 1 Corinthians 6:12-20 that sexual relationships have a deeply spiritual element to them, is crucial here. Our bodies and spirits are not separate entities, and promiscuity is harmful to us simply for that reason. However, in cultures in which sexualised behaviour and pornography is normalised, we can lose sight of this. Moreover, in commercial sexual exploitation the beauty and holiness of sexuality is utterly corrupted. But the wonderful thing is this – no amount of sexual brokenness can separate us from the love of God. There is no story He can't redeem.

Teaching on sexual relationships is important, but it should not dominate our discussions. Far more important is learning from Jesus himself about the things that are important in his Kingdom. It can come as a surprise to discover that Jesus is not as preoccupied with sex as we are! He speaks about it remarkably seldom, and is far more concerned with genuine spirituality, our attitude to money, and relationships with others.

---

64. See for example Bob Ekblad *Guerilla Bible Studies: Surprising Encounters with God* Vol 1 Burlington: The Peoples' Seminary 2019.

Someone who becomes a Christian will not necessarily be spared the consequences of previous actions. There may be people who are far from happy at the change that has taken place, and want to try to lure her back or punish her for leaving her previous life. Broken relationships may still cause hurt. There may be continuing health problems. Don't foster future frustration and disappointment by promising that God will fix all these problems instantaneously. Jesus warned his disciples that they would have troubles (John 16:3). But he also promised to send his Holy Spirit to guide and comfort. Part of maturing in faith is learning to see how God works through difficult circumstances. Take time to pray and listen.

Don't try to control her behaviour. Control is contrary to the freedom which is at the heart of the gospel (Galatians 5:1), and will always backfire in the end.

Forgiving others is central to Christian living, but it is also very difficult – so don't introduce the topic too early. Forgiveness is an act of will, and we cannot do it without the help of the Holy Spirit. It starts with choosing not to take revenge on the person who has wronged us, and we may have to make this choice over and over again (Matthew 18:22). We may still feel angry or resentful, but as we are obedient in forgiving, resentment will

Don't try to control her!

gradually lessen. Do not expect forgiveness to be instant and don't condemn those who find it difficult. By the same token, be wary of "premature forgiveness" – it is hypocritical and damaging to our mental health to declare forgiveness soon after a traumatic event. Allow God to work in your heart and he will bring about the transformation that is healing for all.

Encourage those whom you are discipling to look to others' needs rather than focussing on their own. It is immensely healing to be able to be "wounded healers" who reach out to others who are hurting.[65] A concern to serve others is a mark of maturing faith. Try to foster this ethos of mutual service, and help women to identify the gifts that God has given them.

65. Henri Nouwen *The Wounded Healer* London: Darton, Longman and Todd 2014

Avoid holding women up as "trophies". When there is a "success story", such as Lisa's, it can be tempting to want to hold up the woman as a shining example of what God is doing – inviting her to give her testimony, or using her story in publicity. But this might put her under intense pressure for which she is not (and indeed may never be) ready. It can lead to the conclusion that they have already reached the end of the journey and contribute to a relapse in behaviour if the pressure is too much. Some will be able to handle it, but for many more it will be a step too far. So be very careful whom you choose – if you must choose anyone at all.

BIBLE STUDY

Read Romans 7:7-25

In this passage Paul speaks of his personal dilemma – he does not understand himself. It is his deepest desire to lives as God wants him to live, but he finds that he fails in this, over and over again. Paul is describing an experience which is common to all Christians. We want to live our lives as God asks us to but we find it difficult to do so. There seems to be a constant battle to do God's will and we have a constant tendency to go our own way. We seem to fail over and over again. This results in feelings of shame and guilt – we feel that we have let God down. But Paul is full of praise for he knows that the answer to the problem is not to look within himself for strength to do right, but to Jesus Christ, who will deliver him from his self-destructive tendencies.

QUESTIONS FOR DISCUSSION

> What does being disciples of Jesus mean for us?
> How can we help women in their discipleship journey?
> What does it mean for a believer to become more like Jesus?
> How far does Romans 7:7-21 resonate with your own experience?
> "The God of all comfort…comforts us in all our troubles, so that we can comfort those in any trouble with the comfort we ourselves have received from God." (2 Cor 1:3-4). How can we enable women to become comforters of others?
> Giving example from you own lives, discuss how the Twelve Step programme can be applicable in the lives of all believers.

CHAPTER 15

Spiritual Matters

"He trains my hands for battle, my arms can bend a bow of bronze"

Psalm 18:34

"Blessed are the meek, for they will inherit the earth"

Matthew 5:5

1. Marina's Story

AS THEIR MINISTRY progressed, Tom and Lydia became keenly aware of being caught up in a spiritual battle. There were constant difficulties. They made the painful discovery that a team member had been stealing from the funds – a little at a time, over several years – and had to dismiss her. Local government officials were suspicious of them because they were Christians and sometimes put obstacles in their way, making development of the ministry more complex and slower than it should have been. Above all, however, they found themselves questioning and agonising over some of the women they worked with. Marina's story weighed heavily on their hearts. Marina was a tough, violent drug-dealer who cheated her way through life. The team prayed for her for years, but things seemed only to get worse. When Marina asked for prayer one night, they were delighted – here was the breakthrough they had been hoping for. Eventually she left commercial sexual exploitation and drug-dealing. She had experiences of healing which she herself described as "miracles", but despite this, she never surrendered her life to God. Marina was killed by her former pimp/perpetrator, who missed the money she brought in and her ability to control the other women. The team was heart-broken and mystified.

People who obey a call to follow Jesus and declare themselves His disciples have made a decision to live under God's rule. The New Testament tells us that Jesus inaugurated God's kingdom on earth, but also that this kingdom will only be seen in its fullness at the end times. Believers are caught up in a continuing battle: demonic

Our struggle is not against flesh and blood

powers are hostile to God's rule and are trying to undermine God's purposes. We look forward to the time of fulfilment when God's power will be all in all, but in the meantime, as we seek to do God's will, we will meet with opposition. Paul says in Ephesians 6:12 that "our struggle is not against flesh and blood, but against the rulers, against the authorities, against the powers of this dark world and against the spiritual forces of evil in the heavenly realms." To help us be prepared for this, Paul urges us to "Put on the full armour of God, so that you can take your stand against the devil's schemes" (Ephesians 6:11).

2. Spiritual warfare

There are different ways of understanding spiritual warfare, depending on one's faith tradition and culture. Many western Christians, for example, see spiritual warfare in terms of moral conflict – that is, the constant battle between what we want to do and what God wants us to do. Believers from non-western countries, or from charismatic traditions, are more likely to think in terms of demons and cosmic powers which set out to oppress and destroy individuals and communities. No doubt your team members will come from various backgrounds and will have differing opinions on many theological questions, including this one. The important thing is not to allow your ministry to be hampered or even destroyed because of theological disputes of this sort: agree to differ, and allow people to use the gifts they have been given, with due accountability structures in place.

Whatever our view, it is clear from Scripture that the powers of darkness are in the business of doing as much as they can to undermine God's rule on earth. However, believers have authority over the powers of darkness – because of who we are in Christ. This authority is paradoxical – it requires an acknowledgement of absolute powerlessness and weakness on our part. It has nothing to do with status, wealth or power over others. It has everything to do with the recognition of

Spiritual Matters

our complete dependence on God. This paradox of strength in weakness is demonstrated most clearly on the cross. It was Christ's willingness to die which made it possible for the power of death to be overcome.

When Jesus said the meek will inherit the earth (Matthew 5:5), He was pointing to God's strategy for winning the war against Satan and demonic forces on this earth. God is going to defeat Satan through people who move in the opposite spirit to the forces of darkness. We are therefore called to walk in light and truth, and in humility and with dependence on God, living lives of surrender and gratitude. Satan may be "filled with fury, because he knows that his time is short" (Rev 12:12), but God has the ultimate victory.

The most important thing that we can do to ensure that we are living in this authority is to look after our own spiritual health. This means being part of a worshipping community and practising spiritual disciplines such as fasting and study. Above all, our strength and authority in the world of darkness comes from our relationship to Christ which is grounded in prayer. We MUST take time for private prayer (Matthew 6:5-6), for we cannot grow in faith without spending time in the company of Christ. Most people find prayer difficult, and it is important that we find the way of prayer which is best for us. It may be helpful to experiment with different types of prayer for example, centering prayer or *lectio divina*.[66]

Corporate prayer, with the team, volunteers and supporters, is as much a part of our ministry as practical outreach is. Prayer should be the foundation for everything we do – from starting the ministry (see chapter 3), seeing it established and growing, and the daily task of praying people out of selling and buying sex. Prayer brings people from different theological and denominational backgrounds together as they unite in compassion for others. It is not a case of bombarding God with demands, but the humble recognition that, no matter what systems, strategies and plans we put in place – only God can change lives.

Since Jesus and the Holy Spirit constantly intercede for us, we should do the same for the people we work with in our ministry. Ask God to show you how to pray for people, remembering that "we do not know what we ought to pray for" (Rom 8:26). Take time to listen for God's voice, and "test the spirits" together (1 John 4:1). We often speak of "praying in the name of Jesus", but this is not a magical formula to be tacked on at the end of our prayers to ensure that we get an answer. Rather, it is an acknowledgement that we have no power in ourselves without him, and a reminder that our whole lives should be lived in relationship with Jesus and in submission to him. In your prayer times as a team, if you notice that you are chatting more than you are praying, do something about it. Here is a useful template for your corporate prayer times:

---

66. See for example, Thelma Hall *Too Deep for Words: Lectio Divina* Mahwah: Paulist 1988; Cynthea Bourgeault *Centering Prayer and Inner Awakening*: Lanham: Cowley 2004.

1) Adoration: worshipping God.
2) Confession: acknowledging our sin.
3) Petition: bringing our needs to God.
4) Intercession: Standing in the gap for another.
5) Thanksgiving: expressing our gratitude to God.

Ultimately, though, it isn't what or how we pray that matters but who we are that counts. We must be people whose hearts are oriented towards God. A willingness to forgive each other is crucial (Mark 11:25-26), and a desire for God to change our hearts.

3. Walking in the opposite spirit

The people involved in commercial sexual exploitation (victims and perpetrators alike) are trapped in darkness and enslavement. In practical terms, this means that they are caught in destructive patterns of behaviour which are harmful to themselves and those around them, and they may be under the control of gangs, violent perpetrators or drug dealers. You will see so much of this that you may be tempted to think that the darkness has the upper hand. Yet we must remind ourselves of the truth of the bigger picture – the darkness cannot overcome the light (John 1: 5). Nevertheless, light shows up the things which want to remain hidden and so, as we bring Christ's light into these areas, there is bound to be a backlash as the powers of darkness try to assert themselves against God's rule. But we are on the winning side, for Christ is Lord, and we have nothing to fear.

It is crucial that our teams stand out as radically different from the environment in which we are working. In large part, this will be evident as we make corporate prayer and worship a regular part of team life. But there are other ways too. God is going to defeat Satan through individuals who move in the opposite spirit to the oppression, corruption, extortion and cruelty which rules the world of commercial sexual exploitation, and by standing up for justice for the poor and needy and caring for the foreigner (Ezekiel 22:29-31). We can model the "opposite spirit"

Praying together

by submitting to one another, not gossiping, not pursuing our own ambition at the expense of others, and by being self-disciplined in our sexual relationships and our attitude to money. Walking in the opposite spirit also means being merciful, compassionate and forgiving. We operate in the fruit of the Spirit – love, joy, peace, forbearance, kindness, goodness, faithfulness, gentleness and self-control (Galatians 5:22-23).

Sometimes the need to walk in the opposite spirit will be obvious, and sometimes it will be more difficult to discern. Sheena was an inspirational frontline volunteer who had a wonderful gift of empathy and compassion for the women. One evening Amie walked into the drop in. She was furious because she had just been raped and robbed by some sex-buyers, but she didn't tell anyone this. She just started to scream at anyone and everyone. Sheena went over to her and whispered to her that she liked her and that God loved her. When Amie raised her hand to hit her, Sheena gently put her hands on her shoulders and looked at her. As she did so, Amie began to realise that she was in a safe place and stopped shouting. As Sheena "walked in the opposite spirit" to Amie's need to express her rage, she brought peace to the situation. But while it was easy for Sheena to do this at the drop in, she found it much harder in church, especially with those whom she felt were judgmental and critical of others. Her instinct was to fight back by rejecting people in church who displayed this attitude. But in prayer and with guidance she realised that she was required to walk in the opposite spirit even with her brothers and sisters in church, and accept the body of Christ... with all its flaws and weaknesses.

Whereas the world of commercial sexual exploitation is characterised by lies and deception, we operate with transparency and truth. Rebellion is countered by submission to God and justice. Against the self-loathing which so often cripples the women, we teach a knowledge of God's love and an appreciation of the individual strengths and gifts he has given us all. Chaotic, destructive living is met with orderliness, reliability, beauty and creativity. Lies and cheating are countered with honesty and integrity, resentment and revenge met with forgiveness. We foster an atmosphere of trust, in which there is there is no room for gossip and hateful talk:

> "whatever is true, whatever is noble, whatever is right, whatever is pure, whatever is lovely, whatever is admirable—if anything is excellent or praiseworthy—think about such things." (Philippians 4:8)

Another way of thinking about it is to say that we use different weapons to those who are against us. As Malcolm Gladwell notes in his book *David and Goliath,* young weak David was able to kill the giant precisely by using methods the giant did not understand.[67] To Goliath, who besides his sheer physical presence and strength had the best in modern technology to protect him, David looked weak and

---

67. Malcolm Gladwell *David and Goliath* London: Penguin 2013.

ridiculous. He expected others to act in the same way as him. David, on the other hand, was young, physically unimpressive, and was working without outdated technology – he only had a sling. But Goliath, who relied on brute strength and intimidation and thought that everyone would operate in the same way, was overpowered by David's skill and agility. David "walked in the opposite spirit" and the giant was slain.

As disciples of Jesus, we are aligning ourselves with God in the battle against the powers of darkness. We are called to resistance rather than attack. The author of Ephesians speaks of putting on the armour of God so that

> "when the day of evil comes, you may be able to stand your ground, and after you have done everything, to stand. Stand firm then, with the belt of truth buckled around your waist, with the breast of righteousness in place, and with your feet fitted with the readiness that comes from the gospel of peace. In addition to all this, take up the shield of faith, with which you can extinguish all the flaming arrows of the evil one. Take the helmet of salvation and the sword of the Spirit, which is the word of God." (Ephesians 6:13-17)

Truth, peace, faith, salvation and so forth are the defences God gives us against the powers of darkness. From a human perspective they look ridiculous. But if we persevere with these gifts we will be able to stand firm when evil comes looking for us. The "word of God" is the only sword which we can use to counter-attack, and even then we will be using God's truth, rather than our own, to inflict the wounds. Unlike Goliath, whose armour was made of metal, ours is spiritual in nature. But we must also keep it in good order, through prayer and the spiritual disciplines.

4. Miracles and healings.

The New Testament says that we are to pray for healings and we should be obedient in this (James 5:14). The team prayed for Carly, a beautiful 32-year old woman who had been sexually abused by her step-father. No amount of crack could dull the pain. For three years, they prayed that Carly, who had been to four residential rehabilitation centres and each time had left abruptly, would encounter Jesus. One night at the drop-in, Carly invited Jesus to heal her from those memories. Overwhelmed by the Holy Spirit she received peace for the first time and so began a process of healing. For Carly, the words of Psalm 27:13 "I remain confident of this: I will see the goodness of the Lord in the land of the living", gave her inspiration and hope in her new life.

There is no doubt that God works healing miracles, indeed Paul tells us that some people are given a special gift for healing ministry (1 Cor 12:28). But He heals in various other ways too. As Frederick Gaiser says in his book on healing in the Bible,

> "God accomplishes healing in all kinds of venues and in all kinds of ways. God heals through the work of creation, through the presence of Christ, through the power of the Holy Spirit, and through the prayers and support of the people of God."[68]

So healing can also be done through modern medicine, through the skill of a surgeon or physician. Or it may come through a change in lifestyle – such as healthy eating and taking exercise. Healing can also refer to emotional healing of past hurts. This kind of healing can come through patient listening, gentle teaching and intercession.

We can be tempted to look for healings and miracles so much that we begin to focus on the "gift rather than the giver". Often, God is doing miracles in front of our very eyes and we don't notice it – the transformation of someone's character, the smooth running of the team under intense pressure, people finding access to employment and accommodation.

Always remember that healing ministry is part of God's mission and is a means to an end rather than an end in itself. In other words, it is there to point people to God – not to ourselves (Acts 3:1-15). If healings do take place, be thankful but don't make a fuss about it. Jesus is always low key about his miracle-working; he frequently tells people who have been healed to keep quiet and tell no-one. This may have been to protect the person from undue attention, or to keep the focus on Jesus' teaching rather than his works. Another reason for not making too much of healings and miracles is that it can come as a severe blow if they do not happen. God's ways are not ours, and we cannot expect him to conform to our every wish.

5. Deliverance ministry

Demonic activity expresses itself in various ways. Don't be fooled into thinking that it is always dramatic and obvious. In most cases, it is subtle and easily missed. Jesus' encounter with the devil in the wilderness (Luke 4:1-13) teaches us that materialism, greed and the pursuit of wealth and power are demonic forces which divert our attention away from God's purposes and prevent us from living fully in the kingdom of God. Christians in the west live with these forces daily and can come under their influence without noticing. By prayer and fasting we will keep our hearts oriented to God's values, rather than those of the world around us.

Sometimes, demons do take control of an individual. Specific demonic influence can become obvious during a prayer or counselling session. Signs of demonic possession include:

---

68. Frederick J. Gaiser *Healing in the Bible: Theological Insight for Christian Ministry* Grand Rapids: Baker 2010 kindle location 202

- Complete change in personality
- An apparent domination of the person by an alien individuality
- Sudden change of voice or facial expression
- Flailing limbs
- Destructive violent behaviour
- Physical strength even in frail people
- Cursing and blasphemy against God
- Aversion to divine things

It should be possible to distinguish clearly between mental illness and demonic influence. The person who is demonised will remain sane in his thoughts – that is, there will be no evidence of hallucinations (seeing things that are not there) or delusions (false beliefs which are at odds with the culture in which the person is living). Some deliverance will happen in undramatic ways. For example, during worship, someone may repent of acts of hatred or revenge. However, if you come across some of the features listed above, you will have to get rid of the demon. The manifestation is a demonstration of rebellion against God. But God is still in control. The demon cannot and will not get the better of him.

Never attempt deliverance prayers alone. Always work in a team. Check your impressions with a prayer partner and with the rest of the team. Organise prayer partners who can pray for you while you are working with the person. Where possible, seek the advice of someone who has a specific gift in this area. Don't be driven by panic or urgency – the situation may only appear to be an emergency. There is no formula – the sum and substance is "In Jesus' name, get out and don't come back".

When the demon is expelled, there will be a complete return to normal behaviour. However, in Luke 11: 24-26, Jesus warns that that is possible for the demon to return and for the situation to become much worse than before. In practical psychological terms an example of this could be that, having got rid of one problem, several others can take hold – for example, drug addiction is replaced by alcoholism.

6. Keeping faith in times of crisis and trouble

When we go through difficult times, we have to be honest and unafraid to express frustrations and questions. Like the Psalmists, we can shout out to God with our protests and complaints (e.g. Psalm 88). Talk things through with your mentor and be honest about the questions that are arising for you. Keep praying, individually and corporately, asking God to show you how to pray (Ephesians 6:18).

Be aware of the risk of falling into the trap of a conditional faith. We look for miracles, for answers, and for comfort, and none seems to come. We are tempted to give up on God. But faith which is based only on what we think God can or will do for us is fragile. This is conditional love on our part. God, on the other hand, loves us unconditionally – so perhaps we should try to love him in that way too. If our love for God is conditional, we will collapse easily when things do not go our way, or when the miracles we look for do not happen, or when the suffering around us is simply too great.

Sometimes Christians have a tendency to become preoccupied with demons and spiritual warfare. However, very often, the trouble which comes is a direct result of our own or others' choices and behaviour. Over-spiritualising can be a subtle way of deflecting responsibility away from ourselves.

Even when we experience healing and deliverance from destructive behaviour and disease, we still have to live with the consequences of our actions. Criminal records may stop women getting the jobs they dream of. People who have harmed and controlled them in the past can still pose a threat to women's lives. A woman may long to have custody of her children again, but in the eyes of the authorities she may always be considered an unfit mother. Or she may be freed from her addiction but still have to live with hepatitis or HIV.

Shouting at God

Do not presume on God – never predict that a person will be healed or that a wrong will be righted. These things are not in our gift to know. We must not make claims which we cannot live up to. God can redeem situations, but he often wants us to learn from our difficulties rather than to grant us an escape from them. What we can do is complain to God as the Psalmist does. Ultimately acceptance of a situation, and looking for God's guidance within it, is more healthy than denying that it is happening, or defiance until one gets what one wants. It is OK to express disappointment about the way things work out.

We have to remind ourselves that God sees the bigger picture. He is entirely merciful and knows what is best for each person. It is natural for us to want to escape suffering and pain, and our western culture wants us to believe that this is our right to be cossetted against it – but Jesus explicitly tells his disciples "you will have trouble" (John 16:33)

Remember that from a Christian perspective death is not the end. There is indeed more to life than this. The secular worldview is that there is nothing beyond life, and therefore we tend to try to hold on to life for as long as possible. The idea that someone might die can become unthinkable and so experiencing a death can be a huge blow to faith. However, God has more for us than this life can ever offer, and sometimes to be released from the suffering of this life is a wonderful gift.

7. God has the victory

We will experience great joy at "success stories" like Lisa's (chapter 13) and profound heartache for people like Marina. This is something we must learn to live with, trusting in God's infinite wisdom and perfect love. In Luke 17:11-19, Jesus tells the story of the ten lepers, only one of whom came back to express his gratitude for healing. Perhaps Marina was like one of the nine. Her life was changed for ever by her encounter with Jesus, but she couldn't make a full commitment. Nevertheless, we know that God loves Marina more than we ever could, and we trust in divine grace for her.

In spiritual matters the key thing to remember is that God's ways are quite different to those of the world. We are inclined to want life to develop in ways that we can understand, and which fit our preconceived ideas. However, the amazing truth is that God's strength is to be found in weakness, love is stronger than hatred, and we need not be afraid. We have the gift of the Holy Spirit and even, according to Psalm 91:11, angels who are watching over us. In this spiritual battle, God is the victor – and those who are surrendered to God's will are on the winning side.

BIBLE STUDY

Read 1 Samuel 17:1-50
The story of David and Goliath
Sometimes we can feel that we are confronted by giants – pimps, perpetrators of violence, drug dealers, gang members, child abuse and violence. From a worldly perspective we are laughably unprotected against these things, and there can seem to be little point in our attempts to make a difference. David, who has only a sling and five stones, seems weak, ineffective and foolish. Goliath is arrogant and over-confident, and he thinks David is pathetic. Goliath has physical strength, a spear and expensive protective armour. David refuses to adopt the same tactics; he keeps things simple, and acts with courage and confidence, remembering how God has helped him in the past. Goliath is slow, heavy and clumsy in comparison with David. But appearances are deceptive and it is David who is triumphant.

QUESTIONS FOR DISCUSSION

> What do you think of the idea of "walking in the opposite spirit"? How might that look in your team, and in your personal lives? Can you give any examples from experience?

> What are current "giants" you and your team are facing just now? Do you have any past experiences from which you can learn?

> How do you and your team make room for prayer?

> What is your understanding of the term "spiritual warfare"? Are there any differences of opinion amongst your team members?

> What strategies can you put in place to help you cope with stories like Marina's?

Epilogue

He who began a good work in you will carry it on to completion until the day of Christ Jesus

Philippians 1:6

WE HAVE TOLD the story of Tom and Lydia's ministry – of how it started out as a few people with compassion for the women on the streets and became an established charity with legal responsibilities which is respected in the community. We have noted some of the mistakes and pitfalls, and some wonderful stories of transformation. By telling the stories of Jody, Nell and many more, we have shared experiences of success and growth but also of frustration and failure. We have tried to be real about the difficulties and dangers involved in this work, but also about the joys and delights. Above all, this is a story of learning, gaining wisdom from experience, and surrendering everything in prayer. We hope that it will encourage you to get started or keep going in your ministry, wherever you are in the world.

Much of the material we have presented here is drawn from experiences gained in the development of the ministry of Azalea in Luton, England, of which Ruth is the co-founder and CEO. It, too, started out small, and became much bigger – and the story continues. Over time, the team began to realise that they couldn't just focus on the women they saw in the streets. For they are not the only people trapped in commercial sexual exploitation – sex buyers, pimps/perpetrators and traffickers are just as trapped, and just as deserving of hearing how much God loves them. They, too, need to be given opportunities to "walk into freedom". So Azalea has started up a new but related ministry called "Flint", whose aim is to help sex-buyers walk away from the behaviour which is keeping them captive and causing themselves and others so much suffering. And so another process of learning has begun.....

But the vision is growing. If women in commercial sexual exploitation are loved by God, and sex buyers too, then so are pimps/perpetrators, madams and perpetrators of violence. We cannot demonise any group of people, for every human being is precious to God, no matter what they have done. And if we can reach them, then we can start to transform whole communities, not just individuals. But how can we do this in the increasingly complex world of commercial sexual exploitation? When we first started, at least in the areas in which we worked, things were fairly simple – women were on the streets or in brothels, controlled by their pimps/perpetrators or madams. It was a local concern. Now, things are much more complex. International criminal gangs, working through social media, are creating and controlling highly efficient networks of exploitation, involving not only the women on the streets, but saunas, clubs and escort agencies, and international people trafficking.

Clearly, Christians need to have to have "joined up thinking" too. So it is that Azalea is developing initiatives of networking and collaborating with other agencies. They call it their "360° approach" to eradicating commercial sexual exploitation, and they are finding themselves involved in all sorts of things – collating information for research, raising awareness about trafficking and exploitation in local schools and churches, working with police to stop crime and bring justice to the streets, influencing local policy-makers, and lobbying politicians. In fact, just recently Azalea has been involved in the rescue of trafficked women in Luton and the prosecution of the men and women who were exploiting them. We praise God for the collaboration with the police and other agencies which made this possible, and are excited as to what God will do in the future. Azalea also offers professional mentoring and training, and would love to hear from you. You will find contact details and lots of information at www.azalea.org.uk

Who knows what God has in store as you follow the call to reach out to people involved in commercial exploitation? Whatever it might be, it is our prayer that God, in his infinite mercy and grace, will enable you to bring God's hope and transformation into people's lives and that you yourselves will know His wonderful provision for the task.

Walk into freedom!

Further Reading

Allender, Dan B. *The Wounded Heart* Colorado Springs: Nav Press 2008.

Bales, Kevin *Disposable People: New Slavery in the Global Economy* (rev ed) Berkeley: University of California Press 2000.

Barry, Kathleen *The Prostitution of Sexuality* New York: New York University Press 1995.

Beattie, Melodie *Co-Dependent No More: How to Stop Controlling others and Start Caring for Yourself* (2nd edition) Center City: Hazelden 1992.

Bourgeault, Cynthia *Centering Prayer and Inner Awakening* Lanham: Cowley 2004.

Brennan, Denise *What's Love Got to Do With It? Transnational Desires and Sex Tourism in the Dominican Republic* Durham: Duke University Press 2004.

Brock, Rita Nakashima & Thistlethwaite, Susan Brooks *Casting Stones: Prostitution and Liberation in Asia and the United States* Minneapolis: Fortress Press 1996.

Carson, Marion L.S. *Setting the Captives Free: The Bible and Human Trafficking* Eugene, OR: Cascade 2017.

Carson, Marion L.S. *Human Trafficking the Bible and the Church: An Interdisciplinary Study* Eugene, OR: Cascade 2017.

Carson, Marion L.S. *The Pastoral Care of People with Mental Health Problems* London: SPCK 2008.

Crawford, Christa Foster & Glenn Miles with Gundelina Veazco (eds) *Finding our Way through the Traffick: Navigating the Complexities of a Christian Response to Sexual Exploitation and Trafficking* Eugene, OR: Wipf & Stock 2017.

Ekblad, Bob *Guerilla Bible Studies: Surprising Encounters with God* (Vol 1) Burlington: The Peoples' Seminary Press 2019.

Ekblad, Bob *Reading the Bible with the Damned* Louisville: Westminster John Knox Press 2005.

Farley, Melissa (ed) *Prostitution, Trafficking and Traumatic Stress* Binghampton: Haworth Press 2003.

Foster, Christa & Glenn Miles *Finding our Way through the Traffick: Navigating the Complexities of a Christian Response to Sexual Exploitation and Trafficking* (eds) Christa Foster Crawford & Glenn Miles with Gundelina Veazco Eugene, OR: Wipf & Stock 2017.

Geary, Brendan & Bryan, Jocelyn *The Christian Handbook of Abuse, Addiction and Difficult Behaviour* Stowmarket: Kevin Mayhew 2008.

Gladwell, Malcolm *David and Goliath* London: Penguin 2013.

Hall, Thelma *Too Deep for Words: Rediscovering Lectio Divina* Mahwah: Paulist Press 1988.

Hay, Rob, Valerie Lim, Detlef Blöcher, Jaap Katelaar & Sarah Hay *Worth Keeping: Global Perspectives on Best Practice in Missionary Retention* Pasadena, CA: William Carey Library 2007.

Herman, Judith *Trauma and Recovery: The Aftermath of Violence -From Domestic Abuse to Political Terror* New York: Basic Books (1977) 2015.

Hughes, Dewi with Matthew Bennet *God of the Poor: A Biblical Vision of God's Present Rule* Carlisle: Authentic Lifestyle 2002.

Hunsinger, Deborah van Deusen *Bearing the Unbearable: Trauma, Gospel and Pastoral Care* Grand Rapids: Eerdmans 2015.

Lloyd, Rachel *Girls Like Us: Fighting for a World Where Girls are Not for Sale: A Memoir* New York: HarperPerennial 2011.

Lozano, Neal *Unbound: A Practical Guide to Deliverance* Bloomington: Chosen Books 2010.

Malarek, Victor *The Natashas: The New Global Sex Trade* London: Vision Paperbacks 2004.

Maté, Gabor *In the Realm of Hungry Ghosts: Close Encounters with Addiction* (rev ed) Toronto: Vintage Canada 2018.

Mathieu, Francoise *The Compassion Fatigue Workbook* Abingdon: Routledge 2012.

Miles, Glenn & Christa Foster Crawford with Tania DeCarmo and Gundelina Velazco *Stopping the Traffick: A Christian Response to Sexual Exploitation and Trafficking* Eugene, OR: Wipf & Stock 2014.

Nouwen, Henri *The Wounded Healer: Ministry in Contemporary Society* London: Darton, Longman & Todd 1994.

Patel, Vikram and Hanlon, Charlotte *Where There is No Psychiatrist: A Mental Health Care Manual* (2nd ed) London: RCPsych Publications 2018.

Proctor, Andrew and Elizabeth *The Essential Guide to Burnout: Overcoming Excess Stress* Oxford: Lion Hudson 2013.

Robb, Ruth & Carson, Marion *Working the Streets: A Handbook for Christians Involved in Outreach to Prostitutes* Chichester: New Wine Press 2004.

Rohr, Richard *Breathing under Water: Spirituality and the Twelve Steps* London SPCK 2016.

Further Reading

Saeed, Fouzia *Taboo! The Hidden Culture of a Red Light District* Karachi: OUP 2002.

Sanders, J. Oswald *Spiritual Leadership: Principles of Excellence for Every Believer* Chicago: Moody Publishers 2007.

Sanders, Teela *Paying for Pleasure: Men Who Buy Sex* Cullompton: Willan 2008.

Scholl, Lia Claire *I (Heart) Sex Workers: A Christian Response to People in the Sex Trade* Saint Louis: Chalice Press 2012.

Skilbrei May Len & Charlotta Holmström *Prostitution Policy in the Nordic Region: Ambiguous Sympathies* New York: Routledge 2016.

Skovholt, Thomas M. & Trotter-Mathison, Michelle *The Resilient Practitioner: Burnout Prevention and Self Care Strategies for Counselors, Therapists, Teachers and Health Professionals* (2nd ed) New York: Routledge 2011.

Smith, Holly Austin *Walking Prey: How America's Youth are Vulnerable to Sex Slavery* NY: St Martin's Press 2104.

Storkey, Elaine *Scars Across Humanity: Understanding and Overcoming Violence Against Women* London: SPCK 2015.

Stringer, Jay *Unwanted: How Sexual Brokenness Reveals our Way to Healing* Colorado Springs: NavPress 2018.

Van der Kolk, Bessel, Alexander C. MacFarlane, McFarlane and Weisaeth & Lars Weisaeth (eds) *Traumatic Stress: The Effects of Overwhelming Experience on Mind, Body, and Society* New York: The Guilford Press 2007.

Wallis, Arthur *God's Chosen Fast: A Spiritual and Practical Guide to Fasting* Fort Washington: CLC Publications 2003.

Van Der Hart, Will & Rob Waller *The Perfectionism Book: Walking the Path to Freedom* London: IVP 2016.

Printed in Great Britain
by Amazon